"I AM MORE!"

SURVIVING SURVIVAL

By

Tonisha M. Pinckney

**Chapter Contribution by
L. Da Vante' Pinckney**

www.TotalPublishingAndMedia.com

ISBN 978-1-937-829-57-5

Dedication

"Jordon" and "DaVante'," I love you both dearly. Thank you for allowing me to tell our story. Writing this book was truly a family decision. You are the reasons I had to survive survival!

Without God, I would not be alive today to write this story. I am grateful and blessed!

This book *is dedicated to every surviving victim of domestic violence, rape, incest, emotional abuse, suicide attempts, or any other event orchestrated to end your life rather than fulfill your dreams. You can survive survival!*

Contents

Introduction

Please indulge my transparency…

There was a time in my life that I felt I could not survive all that I had gone through. I felt life itself forsook me. To take it a step further, I thought the singular purpose for my life was suffering. Of course, now I know none of this was true. My journey past that roadblock of despair was a difficult one. Thankfully, I find myself on the other side in a particularly good place.

One day while trying to decide how to navigate what I felt was the worse life could offer, I came to an abrupt realization. What I needed to survive was not what I thought I had to survive! I had already survived rape, abuse, domestic violence, failure, misjudgments of others, oppression, financial distress, homelessness, and various other circumstances and people. I had already LIVED through it! Why, then, was I was trying to survive? What did I think I needed to survive? What did I think I had to survive? Me!

I had become my own enemy. I was internally abusing myself. How was I to survive an emotional attack? How was I to protect myself from an unseen enemy? I had to look at it like any other war. I had to look at myself as any other enemy. How do you win usually? You get to know your enemy! You have to know the strengths and weaknesses of the enemy. You get to know what the enemy is thinking and feeling. For this war to end with survival, I had to befriend the enemy. I had to get to know me. I had to learn to love me. That was the key to surviving me. That was the key to my release from sorrow and pain. I became my own best friend rather than worst enemy.

I knew God created me with and for a purpose. Unfortunately, I thought that purpose and pain were one in the same. By not understanding my true purpose, I thought I was a defective product. When I launched the strategy to champion over the enemy (in this case I was my own enemy), I decided I needed to find who I was before the pain. I had to go back to my Creator (God) and familiarize myself with my original "blueprint." I had to find out who I was designed to be before all the additions, changes, and destruction.

Once I got to know and understand the person I was before the pain, who I am now, and (eventually) who I could be, I was able to realize that I could survive my greatest threat – ME! I confused the pain I was carrying with the things that happened to me. Every minute of every day was a struggle to survive things that happened years before. I was so tired that I felt I could not make it. In fact, I had already made it. I had already survived my past. I had already lived through all those things.

I did not write this book to expose anyone except myself and God. I purposely did not include names of my abusers or attackers. It is up to them to write their own accounts or reveal their own version. This book contains my stories, my truths, as I remember them today. Unfortunately, I could not contain all I endured in this book. I probably only reveal about 20 percent of my story. I hope that what I cover will give you a sense of your own strength as you develop your own post-survival plan. I realized if I could live through all I included in this book and more, I most certainly could continue to live! I survived my own survival!

With the sincerest heart,

Ms. Toni

Survival between the raindrops

I do not want to tell you my story. I need to tell you my story. I want you to feel my story. I want you to understand why the littlest things empower me with the greatest sense of accomplishment. Through my story, there is no intention to expose anyone, but God, I want you to see God's glory in my story. I want you to look within yourself. Please let my survival serve as your awakening. I am not unique in my ability to survive. You, too, have the strength, the ability, to survive survival.

Please extend your emotional hand. Grab a hold to mine. Let us take this journey of hoping, crying, learning, loving, and healing together. It is in our togetherness that we will be able to survive survival between the raindrops of life and time.

Raindrop. These are my thoughts about survival between the raindrops. Raindrop. They fall so fast, but if you pay close attention (and take advantage of every moment), you can live life between the raindrops of a hurricane. Raindrop. A raindrop is a tear. A raindrop is an intolerable event that causes indescribable pain or hurt. Raindrop. A raindrop comes from a place where you have no control. Raindrop. Raindrop. Raindrop. You do not see the exact spot it will land. You do not have time to evaluate the speed of descent. Raindrop. All you see is that it is raining. Raindrop. Raindrop. Survival between the raindrops is much like playing the childhood game of double-dutch with life. You stand on the sideline (Raindrop) and jump up and down awaiting the perfect moment to get in the game. Raindrop. Raindrop. Raindrop.

Once in, you try your best to stay in as long as your legs and internal timing mechanism will allow. Raindrop. Occasionally, you get caught in the ropes. You face the embarrassment of not making it. You feel the pressure and weight. Raindrop. Raindrop. Raindrop. Raindrop. Raindrop. You try again. Raindrop. Raindrop. You may wait a little longer next turn. You know you can - because you did before. Raindrop. Raindrop. Raindrop. Raindrop. Each success makes you bolder.

I have a hard time understanding the raindrops in my life. Life is full of choices. Either I could stand still and get rained on or I can trust God to make me aware of the smallest fractions of time. It is during that nanosecond between each problem that I must make a decision, live up to that decision, and accept the consequences of said decision. I must do all three simultaneously. I must not waste time in regret or fear. The next raindrop is falling, and I must be prepared. It will either fall on me - I will cry. On the other hand, hopefully, I make a decision allowing the next raindrop (difficult time in life) to miss me altogether - survival.

There could be a problem with striving to survive between the raindrops in your life. If you spend too much time praising yourself for not getting caught, for making the right decision, or for living life despite the craziness, you may end up in a worse place. You spend so much time embracing triumph that you forget that you are in the midst of a storm, and the next raindrop is falling. Between each raindrop that soaks our lives, we must prepare for what is to come (good or problematic).

Raindrop. Happiness. Children. Raindrop. Pain. Raindrop. Education. Raindrop. Death. Raindrop. Career. Raindrop. Poem. Raindrop. Fear. Dancing. Raindrop. Friends. Raindrop.
This is my chance, between the raindrops of my life, to release some pain, express joy, and discuss what God brought me through. I want to take you on this journey with me. My journey has had more pain than love, and more silence than laughter. To survive, between the raindrops, I had to hear the

music in my soul. I hope you can hear the music as you read. I hope you can see that raindrops are temporary and that though soaked by the effects of life, you will dry off, and you will survive.

I once wrote in a diary of sorts:

> "I never thought this day would come. The day when I look to God and was still afraid. The day when I sought His face and instead saw darkness. Not darkness as in evil. Darkness as in abyss, emptiness, and lack of light. Space. A place where space is so thick that I see less than nothing. A place where nothing would be a blessing. Darkness. Loneliness. Aloneness! I know God is there – I do! I know He loves me – I do! I know I am His child and I am His own – I do!"

I felt orphaned. I felt like a motherless child, but I had a mother. She did not know the pain I faced. My pain interfered with how I saw my mother – my God-given nurturer. She was just trying to help. In my mind, it is always her way or no way. I felt like if I chose to do anything differently than what she said, she took it as a personal affront. I did not want to go to her church! I did not want her trying to solve my every problem. I knew I was not the perfect mother - neither was she! Shifting the blame, I thought if she were the perfect mother then I would not be so messed up! I would not feel the unachievable need to please others. Those were my thoughts at that time.

When you are in pain, you adhere to whatever thoughts will bring you comfort. This results in misplaced blame, guilt, and reliance on untruths. Pain changes feelings of loneliness into self-isolation.

I grew up feeling as if I could not please anyone. I thought the only way to make others happy was to be exactly what they wanted me to be and nothing less. In order to please others, I erroneously thought, I had to set side my own enjoyment, interests, happiness, and goals. I learned to be a chameleon. I learned that knowing me was a waste of time. I did not matter to anyone; so, why should I matter to myself? Once I became a mother, I thought I was living only to provide love, affection, protection, hope, and stability in the lives of my children. I have never had or felt any of those things. How do you give something you do not have – never truly felt? How does one create without a prototype, idea, or even a picture?

My mother loved me. The events in my life caused pain and scars. Eventually, those scares scabbed over preventing me from feeling the particular love I needed and desired. I mistook the lack of feeling for the lack of love. I was loved. I finally realized I was numb to all but pain – including love.

I often sat thinking about my past, allowing anger and resentment to loom above me. All the while fighting to keep the seeds from taking root in my heart and soul. Even as I am writing this book for you, I can still feel the weight of the past. I can hear the little girl, the blossoming teenager, the newly born woman, the strong lady whisper in my ear …

"No-one one protected me! I was not protected from the first-second –or third rape. I was not protected from a crazy husband that beat my ass. I was not protected from the verbal, mental, and emotional abuse. No one protected me from friends who used me for what I had, who I knew, or what I knew. No one protected me, a pregnant wife, from beatings so badly and so traumatic that it could have led to her son's later mental illness diagnosis. No one protected from me from being used by man after man. No one protected me from the aloneness that is in the black church. There was no protection from the hauntingly sweet smell of my father's last breath. There was no protection from being a single mother of two sons when that single mother has no confidence in men and only knows the hurt of a man. There was no protection from me! No one to protect me from me!"

So I stood unprotected, unloved, unwanted, unappreciated, unwelcome, inadequate, and dark. Many said the ability to "stand" was a blessing. I saw it as my curse. I have never been allowed to collapse – just to throw my hands up so I can fall totally apart. So many things happened in succession; there was no opportunity to stop and dress my wounds. My cries for help received no response. My mother tried to a certain extent. In all fairness, she had my father to appease. My mother's only real mistake was that she never asked what kind of support I needed – for what I needed her to pray. In my opinion, she probably felt she knew exactly what I needed in life and from her. This is certainly no different than most parents. So much that she never asked and either negated or discounted what I told her. But, she tried. I know she did. My layers of pain upon pain, incident upon incident, had to make it difficult to mother me. I am grateful she never gave up. Prayer was her best gift. Knowing that she was praying for me helped me hold on and not give up.

I knew my mother and father loved me. I knew they were not to blame. Nevertheless, I had to blame someone for not protecting me. I was too scared to blame God. Furthermore, I knew I could not survive blaming myself.

I thought:

"How will I move past all this" or rather "can I move past all this?" With every breath, I was starting to believe I could not move on to another part of life. I was starting to believe that there was no man created that is going to give me that hug I need. Nor is there a moment of happiness that will dissolve all the pain. That hurt is unto death. I do not want to die, but did once. The pain was starting to feel as if it is the only lasting marriage I will know. Would I be 70 or 80 years old with the same pain? If I lived that long!"

Now, I look back at all I lived, survived, and these years of surviving survival and am grateful. I am thankful that God never left me. I am grateful that my mother never gave up on loving me and showing her love for me. I am thankful that the church was always right there. I am thankful that I can see past the pain, past the survival, and live my healing between the raindrops!

A Place and a Purpose!

I remember looking around and feeling as if there is no place for me in the world. I remember thinking I was so unique that God must have forgotten to create a place for me to exist comfortably. My thoughts would wonder even further. At the end of my thought trail, I would often find myself in a dreadful state of complete dismay. At that point, I found myself feeling like a single micro black spec on an oversized white wall or a lone star in a clear moonless midnight sky. I realized that I was not making use of the time I had. It was not that God had not created a place for me. It was as if God created so many places and so much space for me, only He could tell me how to utilize it properly.

I was not in limbo.
I was not wondering.
I was not a lone star.
I was set apart!

With this realization came the knowledge and wisdom that I was not better or worse than anyone else, I was just me. I was learning what it truly meant to be me. My skill set was evolving as my faith evolved. As my passion became more intense, my purpose clarified. God knew I needed room to grow. God knew that confining me to a single place would leave me feeling claustrophobic. He knew His creation – God knew me.

I wish I can say I learned this lesson once. I wish I can say once I came to this realization, I allowed my potential to explode leaving marks all over that wall and all over the skies of the universe. Instead, I often drifted back to that abyss. The reoccurring epiphany that I was set apart often brought me to an aloneness, which my thoughts eventually cultivated into isolation.

To have a single place and a singular purpose is hard enough to find. However, to awaken knowing your purpose is dependent on the situation or setting in which you find yourself is even more difficult. Once you find yourself in a new place in life, you also find yet another purpose (reason) for your existence. Your purpose may not be that one thing others recognize as "purpose." Your purpose, in fact, may be a combination of different purposes – many callings – many abilities to develop and cultivate change!

I have met others like myself. You, reading this book, are probably such a person – like me. You fit in everywhere, yet nowhere. You seem to know too much, yet too little. You are constantly seeking to grow knowing you will soon feel you have outgrown where you are, who you are, and those you know. Somehow, you do not feel better than anyone. In fact, you feel less. You envy others who have somehow figured life out. Your life is a thrilling journey filled with tremendous passion and excruciating pain. You spend your life hoping (someday) to fill the space around you.

What I had to do, what you must do, is fill the space within! I realized the echoing voice screaming for attention was not me shouting into the world. It was my inner voice trying to get the attention of my heart, my mind, my soul. I was desperately seeking the attention of God. He was always there whether I felt His presence in my life or not. I thirst for a deeper relationship with myself and God. After I survived my survival, I felt my pain needed a purpose. I frantically looked to add purpose to that pain. Instead, I found that I overlooked my purpose. My pain was part of my purpose – not my purpose – and my purpose far exceeded a link to my pain. I was searching for the wrong purpose – the right answers to the wrong questions.

The hurtful events of my past created an emotional distance. I had not one problem, but two. (1) Living in the vast expanse God provided for me. (2) Loving the intimacy God had created within me. Reminders of my past prevented me from loving or even appreciate that intimacy. Instead, I resented it. I pushed as if against closing walls. Internally, I screamed as if the silent vibration could separate me from the pain. As the space within enlarged, it became more difficult to fill. As the place of torment grew I grew further from the source of my love. I grew away from my ability to feel love.

Love is sensual and sexy. Love is honest and forgiving. Love is righteous and powerful. For me, love was a distant tease. I knew and understood the love of God, or so I thought. What I could not understand was how that same love translated to humans. So the logical, somewhat circular reasoning, was just that I did not truly understand the love of God. The vast space within me had expanded beyond what is acceptable when seeking to maintain intimacy with God. My internal space had grown so much; it seemed to merge with the external space, the world outside of me. So, I felt overwhelmed. I felt overwhelmed by that lack of intimacy. I felt an intense need for belonging.

A different problem then emerged. I was acting outside of my purpose. My creation plan required I am set apart. Since I longed to belong, I began to act making belonging feasible; thus, acting in direct conflict with my purpose. I was fighting two battles that created a conflict – me versus my soul!

As I learned to survive between the raindrops, I learned to create intimacy within as I navigate the immense external space God allowed for me. Surviving between the raindrops, I learned God was my guide, my strength, the source of the unknown love. Most importantly, there were three lessons: (1)

I must lose myself in God in order to find my place(s) in the world. (2) The intimacy I sought would never be found by pushing away pain. Pushing away emotional pain only created greater emptiness. (3) I needed to focus less on my purpose and more on my passion. My purpose seemed to change based on my level of commitment to God. I learned my passion was what linked my emotional intimacy to the amazing vastness of the world around me. God created in me passions. No matter where I was in life or what I endured, those passions never changed. My life surviving survival was my purpose and part of my purpose.

Coming through the storm – The little lady within

When I think of my life, an image comes to mind. The image is of a little girl playing outside in her favorite silver-gray and pale pink dress. She is only in her early pre-teens – may be ten or eleven. The clouds above her head threaten a dangerous summer thunderstorm. She looks up and smiles. She knows the storm will bring strong winds and loud thunder, but she awaits the rain on her skin. The little girl waits for the cooling drops of rain.

As the rain begins to fall, she is soon introduced to more than she expected. She expected gentle cleansing drops. Instead, hail and whipping pelts of rain overwhelmed her. The droplets fell like bricks. The little girl looks down at her dress darkening as it tries to absorb all the rain it can hold. Finding herself in soaked, she fails to realize she is crying. She looks up as if she will see the end. In the sky, she sees a light peeking through endless clouds. Immediately, she realizes her predicament. She is in the midst of a storm. She is drenched.

That little girl's tears have themselves become a hurricane in the midst of the storm. The girl stands up. She holds her back straight. She takes a step. She takes another step, and then another step. With each step, she realizes the dampness fades. The storm is still bombarding her. But, she began to dance. Suddenly, she felt like the rain had no effect on her. She dances. She sings. She walks. She plays. She prays. She cries. The young lady finally kneels. As the storm subsides and the strength of the sun overwhelms her, she hears her mother call in the distance. "Girl, why didn't you come inside out of all that rain? I know you are soaked 'n wet." She replies, "I had so much fun Mommy. While everyone was inside hiding from the storm, I played. I wasn't scared because I saw the sun and I knew it wouldn't be long before the storm was over."

That is my vision of my life. My life is far from easy. I cannot even describe my life as living from one storm to another. Rather, each storm slowly transitioning into the next leaving no time for me to transition, no time for me to prepare. I am that little girl. That silver-gray and pale pink dress was the color of my favorite childhood outfit. I honestly do always behold the sun shining in my life. God always seems to show me signs that in the midst of the worst, there is the best.

I live between the raindrops. I live between the tears. Instead of crying in the storm, a storm I can do nothing to control, I started to think of things I could do to help me manage the storm. I began to develop plans to balance out the pain. I learned to appreciate even the smallest moments in time. Time is space. So much can be packed into even the smallest spaces. Eventually, I grew to know there was more to me than can be contained in anyone else's idea of time. God has His own timing, which is not limited by any clock or calendar. He assigned a certain time and speed for my life.

What another person could do in a year did not determine what I could do in the same twelve-month period. Funny enough, this freed me. I no longer engaged in self-imposed competition between others my age. I found myself comparing less and less the successes and failures of others to my own. I realized there was a unique place called "Survival" between the raindrops. When I lived in the 'more', I was able to exceed my wildest expectations for myself. When the winds of different storms pushed me back, having a sense of timing became more than a redeeming quality, but a survival skill.

There is no way I can continue this discussion without explaining the power of prayer. Just as that little girl, I stopped to pray. In those times of prayer, there is clarity. My perspective shifts from the storm to each individual raindrop. I no longer feel overwhelmed by the dark scary clouds looming overhead. I no long feel oppressed by the massive amounts of water descending on me. I can see each painful strike (raindrop) and navigate my way through even the most dense storms. In meditation, I could see the pace of each problem falling on me. I could see the direction of the wind. Through pray and mediation, I can sense when to take a step. I survived survival by seeing the spaces between the raindrops in the midst of the storm.

It's not Suicide, I'm Just Ending My Life

I must dedicate this chapter to a special woman that I do not remember meeting. She produced one of the most remarkable people I have ever lived to know. Before she made her mistake she gave the world a kind, caring, loving, well just overall terrific individual. My friend (my sister) lost her mother to suicide when she was just a little girl. Through our connection, I realized the pain her mother's death caused, and still causes her to this day. There are constant unanswered questions. This motherless child walks in search of a mother's love. The love her mother gave before the mistake became lost in the pain of her mother's unwillingness to live. Her mother committed suicide. I will not address the story or the issues surrounding her mother's death. That is her book to write. I could not help but reflect on the pain of my sister-friend. I refused to inflict such pain on my children. I thank God for the lady my friend became despite the mistake of her mother.

I even found it in my heart to thank God that her mother's insensitivity birthed a deep awareness in me. I never found it in me to think facilitating my own death was fair to anyone but me. It would not be fair for me to escape what I saw as unbearable -ending my own life. It would not be fair that my ending would cause the beginning of an unnecessary lifetime of pain in the lives of my children. I am thankful for that woman - despite her mistake.

If my friend (my sister) reads this book, this chapter, this sentence, I want her to know that God's purpose for her mother's life extended far beyond the years of her life. To my sister-friend I say, "I thank God that between the raindrops of your life, God created a miracle in our lives. The raindrop imprinted with your mother's name fell bringing life to and nourishing me. I thank you, my friend, for reminding me of your pain. My children will know to appreciate you someday. For that is the blessing for which I am most thankful to God for granting through you, through your mother. I am a part of the purpose attached to your pain."

My Story

Unbearable pain. There are times in my life where my heart just ached. Times that I cried for death. Times when I thought God was punishing me by allowing me to live. I begged Him to strike me dead. I am 36 as I write this book. I never thought I would live this long. I never had dreams that were more than a few months in the making. Thoughts of the distant past: "If I am lucky, I will be dead by then." Or, "Someone or something will kill me by then." It was my hope, my constant hope, to die. I mostly valued life too much to try to kill myself. Is not suicide an unforgivable sin? Well, I am unsure about that one. The lack of surety was enough to cause me to hesitate. The death I wanted was not violent, not bloody. Just death.

One beautiful, sunny day in the summer of 2005, I awoke to realize that I wanted that day to be my last. It was the most beautiful day of the year, not too hot and not a cloud in the sky. Before this day, I thought I was handling life pretty well. I had a few bouts with depression, but I got help from a therapist. I thought I was doing well. The lack of attachment I felt with the church I attended left me open to studying with the Jehovah's Witnesses. I use the term studying lightly. I think I was an annoyance. I loved the debates and the challenges over the Bible I knew and the scripture they believed to be true. I maintained by beliefs as best I could do. That day, I left my apartment with $20 in my pocket and a resolution in my heart. I had a plan. I would go to a pharmacy to buy a bottle of sleeping pills. The next stop was the liquor store to purchase the finest bottle of wine within my diminishing budget. I looked in my purse and found a $10 bill. My first thought - "Great! Now I can buy a $20 bottle of wine and still have money for the pills." I had an appointment with an elderly Jehovah's Witness sister at her home. We planned to have a short bible study, and then just talk. Trying to maintain some sense of integrity and normalcy, I planned to keep my appointment.

I went to the pharmacy by her house and bought the pills. Standing in the Rite-Aid, I looked closely at every brand of pills I could find. I read all the warnings to find the one with the harshest warning and longest side effects. "That'll do it." I do not remember (or care to remember) the brand. I walked to the counter. "I haven't slept in days," I said as I pulled out a few dollars to pay. I knew the cashier did not care why I was buying a bottle of sleeping pills. No one would care. My only fear was that the tears in my eyes would cause her to call the manager. She would not, I figured, she did not care. I walked back to the car feeling as if I had just completed phase one of my greatest accomplishment. I drove to the nearest liquor store in search of that special bottle of wine.

At the time, Zinfandel was the extent of my wine vocabulary. I wanted to try new brand of wine; but, scared I would not like it, I pick up a bottle of Zinfandel. It cost just under $20 bucks. Therefore, after the addition of tax, I would have no money left. I put the money deep in the palm of my hand. I made a fist. I felt the money becoming wet in my hand as I held it tight. I felt my nails digging into my palm. My life and death depended on that last $20 bill. I held it tighter and tighter. It felt like a limp sponge in my hand. Ahead of me, there was a man purchasing a lottery ticket. Why is he taking so long? My long nails dug into the palm of my tightly held fist. I was next. I handed the man behind the counter my bottle of wine. He scanned it. I squeezed the money tighter worried that I had miscalculated, and it would cost more than $20. It rang up as nineteen dollars and some change. Relieved I opened my hand to pay the man. I had no money. The money in my hand disappeared. I know I had just had it. I was aware of nothing else. How could I die? "God, why are you doing this to me?" "I can't do anything right!" I looked around the counter hoping I dropped it. I told the man I would be right back. I walked around the store looking for it. I could not cry. There were no tears left. That was why I had to die. I HAD NO TEARS LEFT. I HAD NO LAUGHTER LEFT IN MY SOUL. Life needed to end. I needed that money. It was gone. Phase two was a flop. But, I knew I would figure out another way.

I jumped in the car angered by my constant failure. I cannot remember much of the trip to the old lady's house – she was in her mid to late 70's. I know it was not far from where I was and in the same town. I know that it took me an incredible amount of time to get there. I remember I could not wait until the meeting was over. I rang her bell. Her husband (twenty years younger than herself) answered the door. He walked me to the dining table. I remember starting sentences but never finishing them. The constantly ringing telephone still echoes in my mental ears. No one was on the phone. The caller kept hanging up. Why did she keep answering? The phone was green; a perfect fit for the 1950's décor. I listened to the song she played on the piano. Classical I think. Its soothing sound seemed excruciatingly irritating.

We talked for hours. I revealed my feelings of overwhelming stress; but, I was careful not to mention my desire to die. I would not make the mistake of telling anyone that I wanted to die. No one can stop an occurrence of which they are not aware. When I had enough, I offered my gratitude and said "Good Bye." I hugged her tightly knowing I would never see her again. One good-bye down. As I was walking out of the door, she called me to her cellar. She said she forgot to show me something. "My husband has a hobby. Want to see?" Politeness said, "Sure." My mind screamed, "Damn lady enough is enough. You've been talking for hours and said nothing. I am on a mission today. You are serving no purpose." I walked over to her cellar door – it was a WINE CELLAR. Her husband's hobby was to make homemade red wine. I remember tasting it at a barbeque they gave a few weeks back. It was fantastic. Most importantly, it was potent as all get up. I felt tortured. I felt relieved. I spent all that time trying to get a bottle of wine at the liquor store and the money just disappeared. God had His tricks - so ok - so be it. She talked for a while longer. All I heard was, "blah blah blah crap crap crap blah blah." Then the elderly lady called her husband to the cellar. My mind wandered, "Am I about to get killed by old people in their basement?" An unexplained smile spread across my face. "Honey can this young sister have a bottle of your wine. She needs to relax." He said, "Sure, that's what it's for. Remember, you must not get drunk. Jehovah would not like that. As a matter of fact - give her two bottles." The old sister dusted off the bottles and placed them in my hand. She wrapped my fingers around the bottle. Relief overtook me - phase two was complete!

With no money and less than a quarter of a tank of gas in the car, I traveled the 20 miles home. I called family and friends with a cloaked goodbye. I wrote letters to my children, my mother, and my friend (my sister). I made sure they knew that no one was to blame. I blamed no one. I never felt I was meant to live a long life. Therefore, I am simply ending the pain. I am simply ending the cycles of torment and torture. My life was mine, and I said it was over. That day another friend, I will call her Tracy came to the house. She stayed with me. She would not leave. My sister (my friend) and Tracy made me call help-lines. I lied to most and said I thought about death but was not suicidal. Suicide was wrong! I was just going to die. No one would watch my children. I had the pills I had two bottles of wine. Now, I have two chicks in my ear day and night! Can I at least die in peace?

It was a three-day process. I cried and cried. Those I told did not believe my pain or maybe they did not understand it. During those days, my friend (my sister) was the jazz to my heart. She told me how angry she was at me. Her anger made me listen. She was angry that I, knowing her mother had committed suicide, put her through this. She was angry that I was willing to put my sons through such lifelong pain. She yelled about my selfishness. I laughed in my head at her. I thought, "Yup, this is the way to get someone to want to live. You yell at them and insult them - this is a unique approach." I pretended to sleep. Nevertheless, she would not shut up! She talked about God. Oh, not the merciful God, she, spoke of hell. I was in hell and found a sense of comfort in knowing that every day would be the same. Going to hell meant I would know that there was never a prospect of the next day being better than the last. In life, my hope died every night.

I mostly slept for three days. I only remember intermittent conversations. On the fourth day, I looked at the two unopened bottles of red wine on my tall dresser in front of my bed. My eyes involuntarily looked to the ceiling. I got up from the bed, walked over to the place where I placed the pill bottle, picked it up, and held it to the sunlight. I remember feeling overly aware of my actions. I heard a voice - "He wants you dead so bad that he has convinced you to kill yourself. He tried in every way possible, but you are still here. DO YOU SEE HOW MUCH YOUR LIFE IS WORTH?" Had God just told me that I was worth something – that my life had worth? I could not cry. I could not say a word. I could not move. Then, I called my sister (in love if not of blood) to ask if she was going to church. That beautiful Sunday morning, I went to church. The choir sang a song called "Jehovah is my God." I heard the pastor preach about depression and death. I heard Bishop Searight preach (seemingly directly to me) about purpose, and God's intentions when He created us. I knew in that moment that I was nothing, God was everything, and my life was worth more than I knew. I had to live to see what I was worth to God, to humankind, and why I was such a threat to Satan.

God chose me. I still cannot say I fully understand why. I came to the realization that if Satan (the Devil, the Enemy, Evil) was/is so invested in my death, God must have invested even more in my life. I cannot kill that. I no longer wanted to die. I no longer felt suicidal. I felt in limbo. I wish I can tell you that I wanted to live. I can tell you that I did not actually want to die. I put my life in the hands of the One that created me. I knew His voice, and I would never forget it. I believe in this moment, Jesus not only saved my soul, He took the time (between the raindrops) to save my life. I gave power to fear. I feared living another day. I felt as if my past would be forever before me. I saw no future – I could not even see God. I felt powerless, hopeless. God gave me the strength I needed to reclaim the power I gave to my past. I became future focused. I not only surrendered my life to God (the very life He gave me), I returned to Him full control over my life. I was on my journey of surviving survival! I have yet to tell you what brought me to that point.

Surviving Rape

At the age of twelve, I was raped by my best guy friend (age 13) and his friend (age 14). They came to visit me at my family's Plainsboro, NJ apartment. My best friend and his friend called earlier that day to ask if they could come play Nintendo with me. I told the boys that they could come over. In a flash of a moment, they had me stretched out on my parents' bed (my Nintendo gaming system was in their room) with a knife to my throat. The two boys took turns holding me down and raping me. I remember catching a glimpse in the younger boy's eyes, even in the dark, even though my fear, I could see his fear and confusion. His friend led him on a devilishly dark path, and I was their first stop. They made me a woman, not allowing me the opportunity to be a budding lady. A part of me left with them as they exited my parents' bedroom window that night. I thought this was the worst thing that could ever happen to me. As the boys were leaving, I asked, "Why did you do this to me?"

That night, I did not tell my parents anything about what happened. I do not know if I thought that I could pretend, what happened would just go away. That whole next morning was foggy. I walked to the bus stop as usual. Saying nothing, I took the school bus as usual – saying nothing. I only remember telling the guidance counselor at school what happened the night before. I do not remember saying any of the words. I do not remember the look on her face. I just remember feeling shame and fear. At that moment, I still could not quite grasp what happened to me.

My parents were called. The police were called. It was obvious no one believed me. However, no one could think of a reason not to believe me. I was a good girl with good grades. The boys had some trouble, but nothing substantial. When all was said and done, the boys received probation. If they did not sexually assault anybody between that time and age18, their record would be expunged. That was the beginning of my feelings of worthlessness, shame, and a sexual awakening it would take a while to understand.

In the months that followed, I did something terribly out of character. I was pretty much an honest child – besides the "white lies" children tell. One day, my mother called from work instructing me to walk to the local supermarket, which was a mile and a half away. It was a hot summer day, not too long before my birthday. I asked my mother if I could get a snack while at the store. She said no. In a length of time that it took to walk to the store, I got extremely upset. For some reason, a sense of entitlement overwhelmed me. I felt I deserved a treat and anything else I wanted. I felt like I was just not getting anything I deserved out of life. That day I went on a mini-shoplifting spree.

After stealing from two stores, an in-store police officer caught me stealing from the third store – the supermarket. He noticed me putting a bag frozen green beans in my purse. The officer looked as if he was going to let me walk away without punishment – as if he just wanted to put a little fear in to me. At the last minute, he decided to check my purse to see if I stole anything more. His hunch was correct. There were quite a few more items in my purse stolen from the other stores. Stupid stuff: Fake nails, silly putty, fake money, a professional calculator, batteries, a few rolls of calculator paper, and I think some candy or gum. I did it up – 13 years old. Things people would call attention-seeking items.

The outcome – my mother placed severe and necessary restrictions over my young life including a restriction from carrying a purse until she gave me explicit permission to do so. The police officers did not arrest me recalling the incident (rape) I recently endured. My father took me to each store to apologize for my actions and tell the store owner how shameful I felt. One pharmacy owner wanted to press charges, but the officer informed him that he could not since no one at the store actually caught me and the police officer refused to say where I got the items. I was banned from all three stores.

I was another kind of stereotype. Surprisingly, I did not feel the shame I thought I would feel. The system did not punish me just as they did not punish the boys that sexually assaulted me. Not too long after, I made a failed attempt to run away from home. Not knowing where to go, I only hid in the basement laundry room of another building in the apartment complex. The only thing going through my mind was whether I would be raped again and whether they would kill me this time.

The following year, my father needed to be closer to our church and hopefully start his ecclesiastical career. I moved with my parents to Orange, NJ. I loved our apartment. It was a spacious apartment on the first floor of early-1900's two family house. It had two bedrooms with elegant dark wood molding and floors throughout. I liked my school. I made plenty of friends. I think what happened to me in the year prior opened me up to life rather than closed me off from it. Not at all promiscuous, but the possibility of my life heading in that direction was certainly there.

Until one day after spring break. I was thirteen. Thrust into the world, I was a tall, rapidly developing young woman with low self-esteem and no real understanding of sexuality. The world proved its power. I was raped again! One year later! Only worse! I was battered, abused, assaulted, raped, and sodomized by three teenage boys in the Orange High School bathroom. Earlier that day, I arrived at school with my jacket. As one of my morning classes was beginning, a girl I only knew by face came up. She informed me that my jacket was in the bathroom. I checked the bathroom, and there was no jacket. A quick look in my locker revealed the jacket not there either. Maintaining my focus on school I went to class figuring I would get my jacket at some point during the day.

The three boys who would eventually rape me seemed interested in talking to me throughout the day. That was unusual for them and me. Otherwise, there was nothing remarkable about that day. Finally, time to go home, I looked for my jacket in my locker, and it was not there. I looked in the girls' bathroom first; it was not there. I frantically looked around the rapidly emptying school building. Classroom after classroom, my white jacket with neon multicolored piping was mysteriously absent.

Finally, checking the last bathroom, I heard footsteps behind me. Before I knew it, the teenage boys grabbed me from behind, forced naked from the waist down, multiple hands on my breast. I was thinking "NO!" – trying to scream "NO!" I could not hear my voice. The 3 young teenage boys forced my head into the sink and "fucked [me] til [I] bled." Time seemed to stand still. The repeated rapes and sodomy went on for what seemed like hours. In reality, it was just about 45 minutes to an hour. I think I remember them throwing my jacket at me.

As the guys were leaving, I asked, "Why did you do this to me?" (This was the same question I asked the boys in Plainsboro as the climbed out of the window. I still do not know why I asked either time.) Almost in unison, they responded, "Because you were there!" I pulled my clothes together and stumbled out of the bathroom – down the hallway – down the stairs – out of the school's front door – passing custodians and teachers along the way. I walked down the street feeling the sheer life was flowing out of my body. Weak

23

and tired, I arrived at my little brother's babysitter who lived about 4-5 blocks away.

Once at her house, I asked to use the bathroom. Bleeding more and more, I called my mother. Remembering, the year before my father called me a "tramp" and a "slut" after that rape. I planned to say nothing to anyone. I told my mother it was "my time of the month." I remember being in the supermarket getting feminine supplies and feeling the blood rush down my legs. Somehow, it was comforting. Once I got home, I rushed into the shower – that was all I remembered. My mother found me face down in the bathroom (she said she called me several times and I did not answer). She walked in to what she thought was a murder scene. Blood was all over the walls, tub, toilet, sink, and floor.

I remember her picking me up and with tears in her eyes saying "Baby, what happened?" I said, "They raped me." The rest of the night and the days to follow are a blur. I remember coming to in the emergency entrance at East Orange General Hospital. I tried to understand the violation of the rape kit procedure. I passed out several times. The last time I remember passing out, I looked in the mirror, in the hospital emergency room bathroom, when the room began to spin. I was thrust into a heavy, thick, lonely darkness. I felt my legs weaken and my heart racing. PAIN! My head struck the sink. I awakened to unintelligible voices and fading images as the team of nurses and staff rushed me through the halls into surgery by a tall handsome older African-American doctor with tears in his eyes. He was the doctor who delivered me. He looked like a father who just found out someone raped his own daughter. My father only repeated over and over, "How could this happen?" "How could this happen to **me**?" "Why, God, why?" I remember thinking on the way to surgery – "Nothing happened to you – nothing happened to anyone but me"

My parents said we were not going to tell anyone we knew about the "incident." It became a lonely journey. My parents did not – could not – understanding my pain or sexual confusion. I felt worthless unless I agreed to sex. "No, doesn't mean anything," I thought. "If they want it, they will take it."

After many months of depositions and a long court battle, the three boys were fully acquitted. They were not guilty, and I was no longer innocent. A lose-lose situation. We wondered if it had anything to do with the prosecutor and judge having lunch with the mayor (up for re-election) every day during the trial. We wondered why the doctors' evidence of multiple internal and external vaginal and anal tears meant nothing to the judge. We wondered how the boys could admit to everything (saying it was all consensual) and the judge believed them over me, my tears, my injuries, my hurt, my fear.

If one could measure the severity of an instance of rape, that first rape was minor compared to this second incident. In the years following, I realized both had a unique power and role in the destruction of emotional and spiritual foundation. The rapes combined with the reaction of my father, the judicial/criminal justice system, media, school officials, and friends created a new foundation. This new foundation supported the framework for a complete lack of self-esteem, self-worth, self-value, and self-appreciation.

That day the judge took more from me than any rapist could take. It was classic revictimization by the judicial system. The judge took the little I had left – a sense of value for my life. In essence, the judge told me the same as the other judge told me almost two years before – The boys deserved what they took. I deserved nothing – especially not justice. The judge took my sense of safety; my innocence lost forever. The judge took my belief that if something terrible happened, the judicial system would protect me. I heard so many stories about too many black boys sent to prison, yet these, these guilty boys were free – to rape again. The entire system, in my opinion at that time, raped me all over again. After two major surgeries and years of therapy, I was still not whole. I had no rights as a victim. I was no one of importance to them.

To add to my disillusionment with life, slightly less than a year later I became violently ill. Uncontrollable vomiting and severe pain required my mother rush me to the hospital. Evidently, the trauma of two rapes a year apart was too much for my young body. Now 15, I listened as a doctor explained that an ovary and fallopian tube were entangled and cut off blood supply. Gangrene was the cause of my illness. I underwent yet another surgery. Post-operative conversations with the doctor (and a few doctors in later years) removed the possibility of having children from my dreams of a fairy-tale future. Not coping well with my past traumas and my home-life, I was now discussing In Vitro -Fertilization and adoption. I felt totally used up and damaged. At the same time, the doctor offered birth-control pills to lessen the burden on the remaining ovary and fallopian tube saying they could give me a remote chance for pregnancy in the future. My mother denied the doctor's suggestion thinking it would lead to promiscuity. The pills would not lead to promiscuity because pregnancy, I was told, was highly unlikely, if not impossible. Removal of the fear of pregnancy lead to the promiscuity.

Domestic Violence, Intimate Partner Violence, Attempted Murder

"Keep your hands to yourself" - this goes for men and women. Hitting is like anything else. You do it once; it becomes easier to do it again. Each hit gets easier and a little more aggressive or cruel. Eventually, he/she will have a long list of reasons justifying his/her actions. The ability to walk away is the sign of a great man/woman. The ability to resort to violence is moral weakness. Once one introduces abuse (mental, physical, spiritual, financial, or emotional) into the relationship, a slow death of that relationship has begun, and it no longer serves a positive purpose for anyone involved.

I guess, when I became an adult, I forgot what my mother told me when I was young. "You do not play fight," she said. "You do not play fight because once a man gets used to hitting you, he's going to get used to hitting you." This was how our relationship started – playful sarcasm and love taps. "Ivan" (as in "Ivan the Terrible") was comfortable saying those things, and then, "We're just play fighting." He got used to hitting me, which made it easier. Eventually, I began thinking, "I don't like this anymore. This isn't fun!" I see many young ladies who go through that. There were no boundaries there. When he got upset, he had no problem reaching out his hand to hit me. Being accustomed to teasing and belittling me, he had no problem saying the words that he knew could break my spirit.

My mother also told me not to talk to strangers. Another lesson I wish I heeded. I met my Ivan on a bus coming from Elizabeth, NJ to Plainfield, NJ one late night after visiting my aunt. I never planned for a long-term relationship with him. At that time, I had a boyfriend at the time who was facing 8-years of imprisonment due to selling drugs in a school zone. I knew my time with that guy was short. So, well, on to the next guy. That chance meeting on the bus lead to an extremely short friendship turned romance.

Music was the most important part of my life. I lived for hip-hop. I loved to write lyrics. I loved the creativity that surrounded me. I was happy with my circle of friends. For the most part, I felt safe with them. In Plainfield, I lived down the street from my soon-to-be incarcerated lover as I shared a house with three ladies I considered family. Ivan claimed to love hip-hop himself. He claimed he was an up-and-coming artist from Newark, NJ. I knew some up-and-coming artists and a few who were prominent. Hip-hop was our connection. That was until the first time I heard Ivan freestyle. It was the worst I had ever heard. I was embarrassed for him, and I was the only member of the audience. I immediately knew he would not fit in with my circle of friends. Who was I to kill a dream? I offered to write his rhymes (raps) for him. That was the beginning of the play fighting. As we wrestled, Ivan told me about his crazy ex-girlfriend and his crazy drunk mother. As we wrestled, he made me promise I would never be like them. I promised. The wrestling stopped. We ended the night with drinks.

When we met, he had three jobs. Soon after, about the same time I got my settlement from a lawsuit, he lost each job one by one. Then, the final shoe dropped. He arrived at my house late one night claiming his mother said he had two weeks to move out. TWO WEEKS! I had only known this dude for about two months. Still quite naïve, I looked at all I had gone through and found it believable that so much could happen to a person in a short time. I spent much of that time smoking marijuana and drinking with Ivan, so I was not as clear as I could have or should have been. It made sense to me. There was not anyone in my world to tell me different. There was one male friend who warned me that there was something "fake" about Ivan. I considered that jealousy. He moved in, spent my money, and the journey began. It was a rollercoaster ride through hell!

Sometimes passionate, other times volatile, our relationship continued. In 1998, I found out I was pregnant. I felt confused and surprised. The doctors told me that I could not have children. Ivan and I discussed the improbability of marriage because he wanted children. I could not contain my excitement. Ivan's cheating and flammable personality subsided for most of the pregnancy. He attended almost every doctor's appointment throughout the first and well into my second trimester. Then, the anger returned. The cheating commenced.

Since my parents were pastors, I felt ashamed about my lack of shame. I looked at the pregnancy as a gift. A gift from God – and Ivan. It was not a shameful situation, in my perspective at the time. So, I silently cried on the nights Ivan did not come home. In the beginning of my third trimester, I realized I did not want to be with Ivan for the rest of my life. He began to talk about marriage, despite the cheating. My parents put pressure on me about "shacking up" and "acting like a family." I knew my pregnancy shamed my parents' ministry. I was unsure what to do. Abortion was never an option for me.

I decided in early-December of 1998 to raise the baby on my own. My plan involved moving where no one, including my parents, would know my location. Ivan, of course, apologized for his actions. He promised, swore even, not to hit or cheat on me ever again Christmas Day 1998, Ivan and my mother arranged for a romantic day-trip to New York City for Ivan and I. I knew he was to propose. I knew I had to say yes. Ivan disappeared for the entire day. I spent that Christmas Day cycling between fear, anger, and intense sadness. Finally, at around 6pm, Ivan arrived at my parents' Central New Jersey home. Cold, tired, and aggravated, I went on the train ride to New York City pretending none of my emotions existed. I was intent on being happy.

We stood in front of Rockefeller Center in awe of the giant Christmas tree, laughing children, sparkling lights, and couples in love. Ivan walked over to a guard. In an instant everyone stopped. Ivan got down on one knee and proposed marriage. I looked around. A tear formed in the corner of my eye. In my mind, I heard my exit door closing and the trap door beneath my feet opening. I said, "Yes." People applauded. Ivan hugged me, no kiss. We left. That was it. He summoned for a taxi, I opened my own door, and we headed back to New Jersey.

The next morning, once again I could not reach Ivan. I found a receipt somewhere in the house showing the purchase of a diamond necklace and a diamond ring. My heart sank. I tried to convince myself that he either bought me two gifts or purchased the necklace for his mother. Nervously, I continued to clean the apartment. I found a small piece of paper with the phone number and name of a woman I remembered Ivan mentioning earlier in the week while on a phone call. I kept the number, but promised myself that I would never call. Hours went by, and I still did not hear from Ivan. Hours turned into the next day.

I picked up the number and called. The girl (barely 18 years old) on the other end was loud and ghetto. She recounted what Ivan told her about me. Ivan told her that I cheated on him and that our unborn child was not his. "He even gave me a diamond necklace to prove to me he loved me. He said you don't mean nothing to him. [Ivan] said you crazy, and you just won't go away. You crazy Bitch!" As did so many times before, my eyes filled with tears. My voice quivered as I said, "But, but…Ivan proposed to me. We got engaged on Christmas." Her response, "You a lying Bitch! He was with me, my son, and my family all day Christmas. You gotta problem. Yo, Ivan right, you crazy!" With that, I hung up the phone.

When Ivan finally came home, he confessed to being with someone else that day. Remarkably, the name he told me was not the same name as the girl I spoke to on the phone. There were two other women, not one. Once again, Ivan promised to stop. He told me how stressed he was about becoming a husband and father. Flowers in hand, he cried as he declared his love. I was trapped. Almost 8-months pregnant, what was I to do?

Ivan focused on preparing for his soon-to-arrive son. He made me feel so loved, wanted, and even adored. The wedding date was set for April 11, 1999, six weeks after the birth of our son, DaVante'. Our wedding was simple. My mother picked out a dress she liked. Her goal was to make sure my tattoos did not show. My father grew distant as the wedding date approached. Just before the wedding, as I put the final touches on my lipstick, my father told me that he was disappointed in me. He told me that I should not get married, and the pregnancy made him and my mother look bad. Tears fell like droplets of fire on my elegantly adorned white gown. As the tears rolled down my face, every word my father said to me singed what was left of my heart. For a moment, I was not numb. For that moment, I could feel. I thought, "You're the reason I'm doing this. Now! You wait until minutes before my wedding to tell me all of this!" I do not remember if any words actually came out of my mouth. In shock, I continued as I sat in the room alone reapplying my makeup. Perfectly hiding my pain, I felt beautiful as I stood at the alter glancing over at my newborn dressed in a baby tuxedo. He, baby DaVante', was all I needed.

The reception was at my parents' house. Non-alcoholic wine, salad and submarine sandwich platter, and a few laughs made for a pleasant afternoon. During the reception, Ivan and his brother sat in the corner with conniving looks on their faces. Soon after the reception ended, we headed back to our apartment with our six-week-old son to enjoy our wedding night. Ivan's sister-in-law offered to care for DaVante' giving us an evening to enjoy. As I prepared DaVante's clothes and bottles, Ivan, his brother, and a friend took a walk to the store. Four hours later, the men returned, drunk.

Ivan pushed me backward toward our bedroom while telling me that he needed to talk. Eyes red, hands clinching my arms, Ivan spontaneously apologized. Speech slurred, he said, "I know you're mad at me. You're mad at me ain't you? Don't be mad. Awww, I fucked up again!" I tried to maintain my footing as he pushed me through the bedroom door. The door slammed. Ivan held my arms as he tried to steady himself against the furniture. His next words changed my life forever. Ivan said, "Me and [my brother] went to that stripper spot up the street. I went to get some drinks for you and me to, you know, celebrate. But, the [liquor store] was closed. So, [my bother] said we could just go in the spot for a minute and celebrate as married men. I didn't mean to Nisha! She was looking good. She gave me some attention. You ain't let me fuck you in like 2 months. It just happened." My body went numb.

Ivan shoved me onto the bed, yanked up the skirt portion of my wedding dress, and forced himself on me as he declared his disappointment in himself. I told him that he was hurting me. I told him to stop. I remember yelling to remind him that I had not quite healed from the episiotomy during childbirth slightly less than six weeks prior. I pushed him off. I grabbed for the sheets. He lifted me and bent my sore body over the furniture. Pain blurred my vision. I gave up! He did not stop until he finished. That was how our marriage started – with dishonesty, adultery, and rape.

Domestic violence, or as I consider it attempted murder, is an extraordinarily dangerous and painful situation for any man, woman, or child. The abuser is attempting to end the life of the victim physically, sexually, emotionally, financially, psychologically, socially, spiritually, or through any combination thereof. "Domestic violence" or even "intimate partner violence" - the terms lack human emotion or empathy. I consider myself a surviving victim. I am still struggling to maintain safety and survive the scars inflicted on my emotional and physical being.

The story I choose to disclose affected my life in an unimaginable way. Ivan did not need and often did not provide an explanation for hitting and belittling me. Now I can say there was no reason or justification. At that time, I bought fully into his shifting the blame from himself to me. Ivan hit me because he cheated or because I was "too good" not to cheat. One of the worse beatings I remember was when I offered to help him get his GED. He said I was "trying to make [him] into something [he] don't wanna be!" That was a hard life lesson. I thought I was nurturing greatness and revealing potential. In actuality, Ivan did not want more. Why should he change? He was pleased with the person he was. I did not err by caring. The error was in thinking he cared about his own destiny. I erred in thinking that improving his value (to himself and the world) would increase my worth. I was not wrong for caring. I cared for the wrong reason with an unreasonable expectation.

One time not long after, I came home early to a double-locked door. My key did not work, and in my heart, my gut, I knew why. Someone was in the apartment with him. I knew who she was. Eventually, the door to our small nicely furnished apartment in a clean building on Clinton Place in Newark, NJ opened. Ivan met me at the door questioning why I was home early. I tried to push through the door, but the door would not budge. I could hear the woman in the background, in my apartment, yelling for me to "give it up."

Determined to get into the apartment, I continued to push. Without warning, Ivan let go of the door. I hit the floor. He and the woman grabbed me by my braided hair dragged me over to the couch. The both of them began hitting me in my face and breasts. I remember hearing, "STOP! STOP IT!" Over and over again I heard the commands. At this point, I was so dazed I was not sure who was hitting me. I just kept kicking my legs and thrusting my arms in hopes of protecting myself. Again, I heard Ivan yelling, "STOP IT – DAMN – JUST STOP!" Was he actually trying to protect me? Did he realize she was killing me? Did he remember I was the mother of his children? "TONISHA, STOP DAMN!" He was telling me to stop – not her!

His hands stopped hitting me. Hers never did. I thought I could break free until he grabbed both of my arms and put his knee on my leg. While he was holding me down, she began to pull my braids out of my hair. RIP. RIP. RIP. RIP. The pain ran through every point in my body. Emotional pain. Physical pain. Psychological pain. So much pain! The man I married held me down while the woman he cheated on me with ripped the hair from my head. My hair has yet to grow properly.

I started a new job at Cushman and Wakefield in Newark, NJ as a temporary hire. I walked in with swollen lips, swollen and bruised eyes, and enough pride left to tell my boss I was in a car accident on my way to work. The cover story continued. I requested time to go across the street to the Superior Court to file paperwork. I had no clue that my story did not make sense. It was time for a restraining order. It was time to get help. When I looked at the photos of my swollen face and missing hairline on the desk of the domestic violence advocate, I realized I was a victim. Until that moment, I had no idea who or what I was. I felt responsible for everything I was living and everything I had lived. Looking at those Polaroid photos, I knew I was in trouble. Somehow, I was lost.

The time he threw Drano at me (which missed me but hit the table stripping it of its varnish) and the night I awakened to a cigarette burn to my chest was nothing compared to this. When I was pregnant with our second child, he made it clear he did not want another baby. Honestly, neither did I – at the time. I was making plans to take our 10-month-old and leaving. I hid the pregnancy test, but Ivan found it. The beatings began. Sometimes, he kicked me in my pregnant belly. Once, he tried to force me to drink rubbing alcohol. He smoked cigarettes and marijuana blowing the smoke in my face. A few times, he held an unwound metal hanger to me threatening to force an abortion. Honestly, many times I wished Ivan would follow through with his threats. I could imagine myself bleeding out – dying slowly. When Ivan stole the food money for any number of reasons, I was be left in the house pregnant without food. Sometimes he returned hungry. Upset that I had not cooked dinner, he beat me, repeatedly. He had issues keeping a job, so the resources most often came from me.

When I say "beat," please understand that I do not mean slapped around. I mean, my eyes were swollen shut for days at a time. My lips were cracked, swollen, and split to the point I could not even call my mother for help. I did not understand how a man could do this to the woman who was pregnant with his child. A BOY! I was soon to be the mother of his second son. I considered giving Ivan sons was a point of pride.

The more my stomach grew, the more he beat me. It got to the point where I was losing more weight than I was gaining. At just under the 5-month point I went into labor. I began taking medication to delay the contractions. I was on bed rest most of the time. I think he felt guilty about hitting me or thought rape would be more forgiving than beatings. I often wondered whether he even cared enough to realize he was raping me. I wondered if he understood the look in my eyes was horror and disgust. He knew about my earlier rapes. He knew most of my past.

At first, he told me that I was "supposed to be a Christian wife," and it was "my wifely duty to please" him. Then, eventually, he said nothing. A difficult pregnancy was not an acceptable excuse. I often said nothing. I am not sure I felt I had a right to oppose. After all, I was his wife. Did I owe him something for "gifting" me with another child? I remembered preachers mentioning that wives are not to "deny" their own husbands. I did express pain. I tried to make my displeasure known. Had "No" worked in the past, I may have been more inclined to protest with more vigor or force. To this day, I am not convinced such protest would have led to a different outcome. I had to protect my unborn child at any cost. I knew he could kill me. I knew he would kill me.

He came home intoxicated extremely early one morning grumbling about how "horny" he was after not getting enough sex before he came home. While I was sleep, or playing sleep to avoid confrontation, he would push his penis in my face – in or near my mouth – while laughing. I will never forget that laughter. I heard it twice before. Once when he poured a small pitcher of red Kool-Aid over my nose and mouth in the middle of the night while I was sleeping. The other time, I was also asleep after an oddly romantic night. That time, I felt him lean over my body. Playfully acting as if I was in a deep sleep, I felt the heat from his cigarette intensify as it moved closer and closer toward my skin. I thought he was just too close. I jumped up as I felt the painful burn of the lit cigarette between my breast. He laughed. There were too many nights as a wife I silently cried myself to sleep hoping I would never wake up.

Hoping God would free me from the hell I lived. There was no safe place – not even in my sleep.

I wrote this poem to express my need for sleep, to rest, to escape, to live. I wanted to know how long before I can be safe and feel safe. How long?

Tonisha M. Pinckney

How Long Must I Sleep?

Hottest of Showers and crispest of sheets
Under the blankets I sleep
I want to sleep until this life is over
Not my life, I want to live on
But, this life, all that is right now, is over
How long must I sleep?
How long must I sleep until darkness fades?
How long before my life becomes a memory
Before it is all over and new life begins
I want to keep sleeping, slumbering
Until my present fades into memories
Until the dreams of the future become my reality
How long must I sleep for that to happen?
Will I awaken in an eternal place?
Will I open my eyes in a distant millennia?
How long must I sleep?
Or, will I awaken next year, next month?
Will my eye pop open next week?
Will the sleep be short, like a nap?
Is it possible I will awaken in minutes?
Could it all be over in minutes?
How long, I pray, must I sleep?
I cannot bare this life!
Yet, I do not wish to leave it!
Sitting as a spectator in the theatre of my own life
I wait for the next act, the next scene
Such an intolerable show
I close my eyes, head back of course
I want to sleep
Awaken me, my friend, when the good part comes
Should there be no more good
Awaken me when it's over

For now, I want to sleep
For now I want to dream
For now, I want to forget now
How long must I sleep for me to disappear?
For my true self to appear in bliss?
Is there no date marked on the calendar?
Is there no suggestion of timing?
How long, I ask, must I sleep?
However long I close my eyes
I will keep them closed for as long as it takes
No sunlight, no moon, will my eyes see
No pain, no joy, will my heart feel
I will sacrifice the beauty to destroy the pain
Believing one day I will awaken
In this very life I am living
I will awaken happy and strong
My dreams will become truth
The hunger will fade
The loneliness will disappear
I want to sleep, slumber, nap
Minute by minute until it happens
How long must I sleep?

    At just under eight months, I went into active labor, and there was no stopping it. While he was in the room, he got a phone call from his girlfriend. Yes, girlfriend. I knew who she was. He said, "I am waiting for this Bitch to finish having this baby so I can leave. I wish I could leave now." He left without kissing me or the baby. I did not see my husband – the father of our second child - for days. He did not even know his newborn son was on a ventilator and respirator in the NIC-U (Neonatal Intensive Care Unit) for days. I will tell you more about my son and how he turned out in another chapter.

The abuse went on for years. I often fought back, or at minimum I tried. When I did he would try to claim I was abusive to him. A pamphlet I read during an emergency room visit explained the various types of domestic violence. The pamphlet discussed what I now know as mutual intimate partner violence. Unfortunately, the author was not clear on the difference between two people abusing one another and one of the parties fighting back for defense or survival. I fought back less and took more abuse.

I chuckle as I remember a time I gathered all the clothes I purchased for him, took them outside in the middle of a Saturday afternoon, and tried to light the clothes on fire in front of all those on my block. Earlier that day, he beat, choked, and dragged me in front of the very same neighbors. Afterwards, he made a call and was quickly picked up by a woman. I was embarrassed, to say the least. Not realizing my lips were swelling, I felt I had to make a grand gesture to save face in front of my neighbors. The fire never actually caught on. One of the items I purchased was a leather coat. When I put it at the top of the pile, I did not know it would hamper the flames. I do not think I will ever forget the clapping and cheering from my neighbors on the block that day. My community gave me strength. When he came home, I did not let him in. I felt empowered. Until…

My September 11, 2001

I think I can safely say America will always remember the terrorist attacks of September 11, 2001. That day left an impact on my life for many reasons. Safety is important. That day many Americans felt their sense of security ripped from them. In response, they clung to families, friends, and clergy for support. We sought assurance that this will never happen again. In the midst of all the national security questions, dealing with the loss of loved ones and property, and fear for one's financial future, life still had to continue.

Upon my arrival at work, my boss told me that my permanent employee contract was approved and ready for signature. A wave of pride overwhelmed me. I had a career. Ivan could not take it away. Despite my arrival with a battered face on my first day at Cushman & Wakefield, my supervisors saw my potential, my drive. I sat at the table awaiting the team to come in and congratulate me.

As I picked up the pen to sign, a man burst into the mid-sized conference room with a television on a rolling cart. He plugged in the television as scenes of panic, fire, smoke, and falling debris took over the airwaves. The pen fell from my hand and tears filled my eyes. My boss began yelling, "I can't believe this!" Essential personnel began running to the roof of the Newark, New Jersey high-rise building. Somehow, I was swept up in the rush. I stood at the top of the building speaking with my co-workers about the probable lives lost. All of a sudden, there was another burst of smoke across the horizon – another plane hit the remaining of the Twin Towers in New York City.

Fear gripped our beings as we stood speechless and unsure of what we just witnessed. As Nicole Simpson, a 9/11 survivor, stated in her book, *9/11/01 A Long Road Toward Recovery*, "I don't think that any of us realized that hearing the stories of people's remains being identified every day would take its toll on us. We could not fathom that seeing the buildings we worked in as a big pile of rubble would hurt so tremendously. We weren't prepared for the political rhetoric that would follow because to us the experience was real. People lives were at risk; and we had feelings, scars, negative images to adjust to, and sleepless nights" (p. 15).

The news of the destruction's attribution to terrorism led to a high alert for the city of Newark. People flooded the streets as they attempted to get home to their families. Rumors of pending attacks instilled more fear on an already confused and terrorized city. I sat next to my co-worker as she told me about an argument she had with her ex-husband that morning. He wanted to reconcile. She also wanted their family back together, but she figured she would "make him work for it." Their conversation ended with him expressing his love. My co-worker cried as she told me that he told her of his continued love and that there was no need for her to worry. He informed her that he had a one million dollar life insurance policy on his life just in case something happened. I do not remember what she said, but I do remember the gut-wrenching cry that followed. My attention turned to my family, my sons, and husband.

Call after call, I could not get in touch with Ivan. Eventually, the company allowed me to go home. I picked up our sons from daycare and continued to try to call Ivan. I was distraught. I was worried. I was scared. He was often in New York, so I was not sure if he was trapped under rubble somewhere or suffocating from the thick soot filling the New York sky. Finally, Ivan returned my call. Without a "Hello", I heard, "What the hell do you keep calling me for?" I tried to explain the situation, my fear, and my concern for him. "Bitch, just wait until I get home!" At that moment, I realized all the terror Americans fled to their homes to escape existed in my home. There was no safe place for me.

Late that night, once he finally arrived home, Ivan showed his displeasure all over my face. Like so many other times before, he informed me that he was with another woman as he tightened his hands around my neck. I was terrified. The arguing and hitting were less severe than in the past or in the future. But, the emotional scars were deep. In the months that followed, the terms "terrorism" and "domestic terrorism" were the main themes of almost every conversation ranging from anchors on news stations to drug dealers at bus stops. For me, I had to reconcile the conversation with my co-worker, the insanity of a terror attack against America, and knowing that there was no place to hide. It was not fair that my co-worker lost her loving ex-husband whom she loved, and my husband lived to abuse another day. I am not sure whether I felt more disillusioned by her loss or my life.

Not Again…Again!

I was in a unhealthy mental space. I was sad (not depressed), scared, and panicked due to the situation with Ivan. We were in the midst of one of the between times. I felt I had the courage to reclaim my life. Recovering from mental and physical injuries imposed by Ivan after an argument, I turned to "Lesley," a distant cousin of my father (stepfather). Lesley and I forged a relationship at a time when we both were facing husband issues. Lesley, who fights with illnesses related to Lupus, had a "live fun and free" philosophy. That attitude was what I needed at that point in my life. I needed to feel happy and free.

Lesley's mother was kind enough to babysit her grandsons and my boys whenever Lesley and I went out. It felt so good to have a friend, someone who understood, and someone who did not judge. Lesley was that person. To this day, I am not sure I would have survived that time without Lesley as a distraction. We often bonded over drinks. She opened me up to a world of people I would not have otherwise met. I enjoyed individuals who were hard working by day and played hard on nights and weekends. Having a sitter (Lesley's mother) at our dispose helped. She was an opportunity to escape.

One night, I got a call to go over to Lesley's house. Growing tired of all the nights out, I told Lesley that I wanted to stay home with my boys, and rest. She insisted that she needed to get out. After all, what harm was there in just one drink? My wall of determination crashed, and I agreed. I got a neighbor I trusted to watch my boys. Lesley told me to join her at a lodge in East Orange, New Jersey. It was after 10pm by the time I reached the Lodge. (I am sure this account omits some details and observations. You will soon realize why.) As Lesley tried the locked door, I had an uneasy feeling. A tall, large bodied man apparently in his early 30's opened the door smiling. He introduced himself; I do not remember his name or face.

The place was dark and empty, a dark, empty bar. I remember the area had a large interior in contrast to its extremely small almost hidden entrance. Lesley and the man walked way whispering. I knew they were making plans, and was trying to prepare my excuse to leave. To add, another uneasy feeling gripped my insides. The front bar, where I sat uncomfortably, had dim lighting. In the rear, the lights slowly faded against the plush red decor, dimming to total darkness. Was there someone else there? What was in the back? I looked for exits. I noticed only one – the front door. If something happened to Lesley and I, we would not be able to get away, to get out. The tall man locked the door just as we entered. No key – no exit!

After a long period of whispering and chuckling, Lesley walked over to the bar where I sat awaiting further information. She sat awkwardly close on the barstool next to me. The man walked over and offered to make us drinks. I declined. Lesley insisted. I accepted. Fear rose. I ordered my go-to drink, Vodka with cranberry and orange. Lesley, giddy, apologized for the closed bar. She explained she confused the nights. Excited, she told me of a pool party happening that night. I sipped my drink. As Lesley spoke, I heard less and less. I could see her mouth moving, but the spinning, tilting room commanded my attention. I prided myself in my high tolerance for alcohol. I never felt this way from a single drink, which I had not yet finished. Lesley never stopped talking. Well, not until another man, tall, emerged from the darkness. I remember thinking, "I thought someone else was here."

Suddenly, it was decided that we should leave. As I stood, I realized, walking was a difficult feat. I staggered, stumbled, and tried to focus as the small room randomly grew larger and smaller, narrow and wider. When I entered the establishment, it took me less than a minute to get from the door to the bar, conversation included. Now, that same distance seemed to take hours. I have no idea how long I was in there. I remember Lesley telling me everything was going to be all right. She seemed as intoxicated as I did. I worried about her. Was she worried about me?

Obviously too unstable to drive, Lesley suggested that I ride with the strange man who to this point was silent and not introduced. She chose to ride with the large man who served the drinks. I did not want to ride with a stranger. I could not drive. I was not clear-minded enough to think through any other options. I noticed the tall, muscular man had on an official looking uniform. This gave me a sense of security, and I agreed. The ride to the West Orange estate was unusually long. I tried to maintain a conversation, but I know I was fading.

I awoke to a deep voice announcing our arrival at the undisclosed destination. We were at the rear entrance of a huge mansion. He helped me out of the car and pointed me in the direction of the beautiful in-ground pool. The water glistened under the lights. Laughter filled the air. The uniformed man held my arm too tightly as he suggested I go for a swim. It was more of an order than a suggestion. Too embarrassed to tell him that I could not swim, I stated the obvious, "I don't have my swimsuit." SPLASH! I was pushed into the pool. Thrashing around, sobriety, clarity, and finally fear gripped me. At one point, I stopped fighting. I chose, momentarily, to give in and die. Just as I again began to fight, a young woman (about my age – 27) pulled me up. That first breath was both freeing and devastating. The reality of the night set in. Staggering around, sobriety and clarity once again fading, I asked the man for a bathroom. He pointed in the direction of a poolside restroom as he offered me his t-shirt to cover up. Despite my last sexual assault being years in my past, I still maintained a phobia of using a public restroom. There were so many people in the house, strangers, the poolside bathroom felt no different from the restroom at a mall.

Moments later, I heard a knock at the door. I informed the person I would be out shortly. As I tried to stand, I could not remember whether I locked the door. I thought, "Yes, I locked it. I remember locking it." Still suffering from the effects of the earlier drink, I was too foggy to realize I had not properly locked the door. The tall, muscular man in a police-type uniform pushed his way into to the bathroom. He forced my skirt upward, pulled my panties to the side, bent me over the sink (reminiscent of the sexual assault at age thirteen), grabbed my hair, kissed the back of my neck as he forced his manhood between my clinched thighs. I have no idea how long the ordeal took. It seemed to last forever. I remember thinking, "Just think of something else – anything else." My mind wandered to scenes from the first rape and the second. "No not that, I thought." I chose to think of my children. I envisioned my boys playing. All I wanted to do was go home to my boys. I thought there was nothing left for anyone to take from me. I was wrong. Too stunned to scream and too numb to cry, I endured it just as I had years prior, just as I had with Ivan. It would be a long time before I would cry again.

When it was over, I stumbled out for the poolside bathroom looking for Lesley. The people at the party looked different. The attendees seemed different from those when I first arrived at the party. As I opened the large sliding glass door providing entrance into the mansion, my intrusion startled the half-naked women and well-dressed men inside. I quickly turned, and began calling for Lesley. Out on the street I saw a familiar face. It was the first man from the bar. I asked him if he had seen

Lesley. His said something like, "Seen her? Yeah, I just finished with her. Now, she's in the van with my boy." He walked passed me laughing. As I approached the van, Lesley stepped out giggling and smiling while fixing her clothes. Was she in the van willingly? Indeed.

I grabbed her and told her that I needed to leave. We needed to leave, immediately. Things become unclear again at this point. I recall trying to tell Lesley what happened. Then, I remembered we had no way home. Lesley summoned the man from the bar, the one who served the drinks, to drive us to my car. That is where my memory ends until later the next day. Still numb from the prior night's event, I drove to Lesley's house. I nervously told her the details. She seemed sympathetic. She seemed to understand. She seemed fake. Somehow her reaction did not offer comfort.

Lesley asked the normal questions such as, "Do you want to tell the police?" But, the questions preceded other less supportive questions like, "Didn't that guy have a police uniform on or something like that?" I never reported the attack and did not speak about it again for several years. After the conversation with Lesley, I came to the following conclusions: (1) No one would believe me. After all, the criminal justice system was not particularly responsive in the past. (2) Lesley settled much of the plan before we arrived at the Lodge. (3) Allowing Ivan back into our lives was a necessary step. I returned, briefly, to my abuser in order to feel protected from the world. At least at home, I knew the man raping and abusing me.

Why do victims stay?

The most common question is: "Why don't they just leave?" Those who are fortunate enough not to have lived through or with domestic violence (or intimate partner violence) could not imagine the emotional and psychological difficulty of voluntarily breaking the bonds between a victim and their loved and respected offender. Their wife or husband, mother or father, spouse or partner, son or daughter, sister or brother, aunt or uncle, or even a grandparent is their offender.

In addition, there is shame attached to the terrorism taking place in the home. The victim is often too embarrassed to tell others they about the abuse. They may think they are solely responsible for the hitting, yelling, belittling, aggression, or other suffering they experience. If enough time goes by, victims may begin to appreciate their abuser for "keeping them in line" or keeping them "grounded." In my case, I even began to see Ivan's abuse as a sign of love. When failed to hit or yell at me, I asked him what was wrong with him. Concerned that his lack of abuse meant waning love, unease existed even in the most peaceful moments.

There are many reasons why a victim refuses to leave. Below are a few I found in speaking with present and prior victims:

- Fear of a new life on their own
- Shame
- LOVE - Misunderstanding of what love is, how love feels, and how love should behave
- Marriage vows ("obey", "until death")
- Religious beliefs
- Fear of sanctioning from the church or religious group, "going to hell", receiving "harsh judgment"
- Fear that their abuser will kill them if they leave

- Concern the abuser may remove or harm the children (or pets)
- They have nowhere else to go
- Fear of abandonment and lack of support from family or friends
- Financial dependency
- Loss of social status and respect in the upscale community
- Ramifications to their career
- Not considering the actions of the abuser as true "abuse" (justification)
- They do not want to be considered a victim
- Family/friend/clergy telling the victim they should "work it out" or "act appropriately"
- Staying for the children or because of pregnancy
- The attacks are far apart, and the abuser promises never to do it again
- The "great" times are extremely enjoyable so to have extremely bad times should be expected

The items listed are not acceptable reasons. Victims use them as rationalizations to stay in abusive intimate partner relationships. Instead of attacking the victim by telling them how stupid they are for not leaving, support them by reminding surviving victims of their strength. Instead of telling victims they have low self-esteem (they know it already), help them actively invest in themselves apart from the abusive relationship. Most importantly, support their decisions. Let them know you are there for them. The victim needs to know that they have someone to turn to when the time comes that they choose not to stay.

No one (not even you) can make a victim leave his or her offending partner. Even when they choose to leave, they may return at least once – if not several times. Ultimately, they must choose. They need to feel the freedom and love not provided within the abusive relationship. Intensive force or intimidation to leave can be confused as oppressive and abusive in itself. Love them to life.

If you are a victim, realize your life is your own. Retain control over your life. It is up to you to survive. The road may be difficult and long. There will be tearful and fearful moments. The memories, good and bad, will flood your mind. That is all a part of the process. THEN, one day you will open your eyes and see what it is to live. You see what your body is like free of fresh bruises. You will begin to embrace compliments. You will open your heart to feel love in its pure state. You will trust again. You will feel worthy of love, respect, and adoration. You will know that your intelligence is power and not a weakness. The first step out of the door is the hardest. Every step you take from that moment on is freeing. Walking out on abuse is walking into a greater quality of life. When you walk out you do not lose everything – you capture everything – more than you could imagine.

Examining the Church's Response to Domestic Violence

So many times throughout my marriage, I wanted to leave. I felt I was not strong enough to leave. I went to different pastors and church leaders and received damaging advice. I was told to "stay and pray." I was reminded of the vows I made. A few times, various people scolded me for "marrying outside of the will of God." Often, I came to church with bruises and sunglasses hoping I got a simple "Are you okay?" Instead, I heard nothing.

People who "cared" aggressively questioned my not leaving. Well, it is much easier to answer why I stayed. To me leaving was not actually an option. After all, I did say "until death do us part." Many nights, many days, I prayed for death. I did not realize I had begun a slow death on the inside. He was murdering me from within. There are many ways that the church helped me through my process, and there are many ways that the church hindered my development process. Ivan used religious abuse to further his agenda to keep me oppressed by intimate terrorism. He was using my faith to keep me tied to him. Ivan often said, "You can't leave because you're saved!" Almost as if staying in an abusive marriage provided proof of my faith in God and my dedication to the church.

I went to a Bishop and his wife to inform them of what was going on. The wife said, "You need to pray through it, you don't leave." The Bishop added, "You made vows, you're supposed to stay until death do you part." That ending term resonated in my head every time he hit me. "Till death do us part!" That line kept me in the relationship. "Til death do us part!" It oppressed me. "Til death do us part!" The phrase chipped away at the residue of my self-esteem. I thought, "I'm really hoping that he actually kills me this time just so I don't have to go through it." Once, I asked my mother why the Church believed God forgives a murderer (a woman who killed her abusive husband), but punish that same wife for divorcing that abusive husband.

In 2011, I did an Examiner.com article series on domestic violence. One of the people I interviewed was Dana Rankin. Dana's husband was a church leader. She experienced a similar situation. She said, "I felt like I just wanted to die. I even got on my knees and prayed, 'Lord just take me away from here and put my children with my parents, because it has to be better than this.' Because it was just continual, sometimes the yelling would be for hours." While Ivan was a not heavily involved in the church, he knew how to use the church against me – my beliefs against me. Similar to Dana, he taunted me.

In speaking with Dana, she described similar reactions by church members as those I experienced. Dana said, "They said [to me], 'You have to pray more with him.' Which he would not, he refused. It was based on my lack of faith, this one particular church stated it was my lack of faith that the Lord would change him, that's why he wasn't changing, that's why the situation wasn't changing. When I would come to church and talk to them, they would just say, 'You just have to wait it out, you just have to see when the Lord is going to do this.'" Leaving was not encouraged; therefore, not an option for Dana or me. No one expressed the need to take our children to safety. Two different families in different churches in different states, we face the same sense of betrayal by the Church. Dana and I were strong enough to understand that God is larger than the Church. God understood our pain. We now work to educate the Church, so that other victims are not faced with the spiritual and emotional decision to stay in abuse or leave the church. We sought out and found church people who were sensitive enough to offer the church as a place of refuge and strength.

I am not including this in the book to bash the church. I love the church! I love God! I am hoping to bring awareness to the need to support victims of domestic violence. Churches must take the "safety first" approach. Clergy must be aware that victims are not martyrs for the Faith. The goal must be to help the victim to live long enough to become a surviving victim – a survivor. It is the Church's job, in general, to help victims (male or female) get to safety and then to move forward to survive survival.

The Church must differentiate counseling from opinion. Any church that would tell you that the Bible requires you to stay in an abusive situation must seriously rethink their understanding of God and His love. The Bible requires we treat our bodies as temples, as vessels of God. Why would God want us in a situation where our bodies are being abused? Why would God want our minds broken down? Why would God desire for us a life of turmoil and terrorism? Is God not the provider of perfect peace? Is He not the Great Protector?

There are churches that know and understand how to educate others properly about the Bible. They understand that God does not want you in that predicament. You did not do anything wrong. You did not do anything that you would deserve such treatment. I did not deserve it!

Domestic Violence in Upscale Circles

My life, during abuse, was far beyond the world classified as "upscale." However, as a pastor's daughter, I experienced many of the fears and emotions consistent with a victim of upscale intimate partner violence. I did not want my life to reflect badly on the position of my parents or my position as their daughter in the church community. Most of those who knew did not discuss the abuse I endured. Others simply did not know due to the veil of silence that existed.

Nationally known as the leading expert on domestic violence among affluent people, Dr. Susan Weitzman appeared on Oprah and other key media outlets. Susan Weitzman, Ph.D., L.C.S.W., is a psychotherapist, educator, researcher, national lecturer, litigation consultant, and the author of Not To People Like Us: Hidden Abuse in Upscale Marriages. Dr. Weitzman heads a Chicago-based not-for-profit organization called The Weitzman Center. She coined the term "upscale violence" in 2001.

Upscale violence encompasses victims and surviving victims of domestic violence whom society considers high profile, well-educated, extremely successful, celebrity, or any combination thereof. Though victims of abuse should not be treated differently based on their income, education, or status level, is clear that socio-economic bias hampers victim support. To add to the difficulty, women who are the recipients of upscale violence are unique in how they experience abuse and the related effects on their self-esteem. Interacting with women in various upscale careers and communities, I found that they face decidedly different obstacles than that of the non-upscale victim of violence.

Dr. Weitzman says, "These women typically have not had any experience with abuse in their background, in their peers, in their neighborhood...Most of these women are typical Type A's. They are go-getters. They make things happen." Used to being in control of situations, the women desperately try to fix the problem in the home. This only exacerbates the situation. They feel a strong sense of shame and responsibility for "letting it happen." Most concerning, they feel as if they are alone in their pain and are often correct. They have no recourse but to focus on trying to survive their abusers, not because they are any different, but for the simplest reason – to too many, they do not count.

This is not to say people do not care about upscale victimization. Such victimization is hard to quantify; thus, people sometimes do not sympathize with this segment of victimization. The extremely low rates of victim reporting victims coax researchers and the public into believing that upscale individuals are at a lower risk for intimate partner violence as compared to their lower income counterparts.

Dr. Weitzman's work and research challenges many statistics and theories set forth by other researchers and organizations in the field. For instance, while the National Coalition Against Domestic Violence reports "30% to 60% of perpetrators of intimate partner violence also abuse children in the household," Dr. Weitzman's "evidence based [unofficial] clinical research" on hundreds of cases found "typically children are extensions of the guys; they are not going to want to hurt the children." Dr. Weitzman was extremely careful during the interview to relay that her findings are limited to those who would fall within the classification of upscale violence. This is an extension of what Dr. Weitzman refers to in her book (featured in chapter 7) as "narcissistic rage." The upscale abuser feels entitled to superior treatment that supersedes the bounds of the law. His children are a part of him; thus, the children are not viable candidates for victimization. However, children do experience direct effects of domestic violence by way of watching the on-going abuse of a parent by another parent. While Ivan was not an "upscale abuser," as defined by Dr. Weitzman, he maintained an elitist view of himself and my family's position in the community (both tangible and spiritual).

"The narcissistic person often feels that society's rules do not apply to him [or her]." (Weitzman, p. 155) As skillful manipulators, they begin to utilize the system which should hold them accountable for their actions to further oppress the victim. Lengthy court battles, exorbitant fees spent on legal defense knowing the victim's limited financial resources, and numerous child custody, support, or visitation proceedings further facilitate the emotional and economic abuse. Often the narcissistic abuser requests hearings and do not show or requests numerous adjournments.

Jan Langbein, Executive Director of the Genesis Women's Shelter, 27-year member of The Junior League, and the Senior Policy Advisor at the Office on Violence Against Women at the U.S. Department of Justice spends time with abused women of all income levels. Jan says, "Whatever she needs, and wherever she is, we will get her what she needs." When discussing Dr. Weitzman's word portrait of the narcissistic abuser embarking on narcissistic rage, Jan pointed out the use of children and pets as a form of control. In essence, the children, pets, faith, and financial security all become weapons of opportunity. As with any crime, the offender is more likely to use what is immediately available to inflict the most harm. For the upscale abuser, there are more weapons available. When it comes to the children, there is a delicate balance for the abuser. The child is both an extension of the abuser and a weapon of opportunity through whom the narcissistic rage can be unleashed.

Jan works diligently against the stigma placed on many domestic violence shelters. Upscale women especially, may not take advantage of such services because they have the vision of an unkempt place with wall-to-wall cots, loss of privacy, and fear of sexual or other abuse. Unfortunately, many confuse domestic violence shelters with homeless shelters resulting in a similar stigma of hopelessness and despair.

How do women get help? How do they get away? Where do they go once they leave? How do they take care of themselves and their children while trying to build an entirely new and safe life? These are all the questions Genesis Women's Shelter answers in Dallas by connecting women with services which address their immediate needs and concerns for safety. According to the website, Genesis' outreach counselors see an average of 1,000 women and children each year, and houses 650 women and children annually.

Dr. Weitzman offers a weekend retreat for more intensive treatment to help educate, strengthen, transform, and empower victims of upscale violence. Healing the Battered Heart© Retreats and Professional Training Seminars offered by Dr. Weitzman and the Weitzman Center are the perfect upscale compliment to service based organizations such as Genesis Women's Shelter. Healing and survival require the use of all tools available. Most often, needed tools are not available in a single location. As a victim finds themselves in different phases of healing they will seek out support necessary for each stage., The key is to start somewhere. Start by choosing to say, "I AM MORE!" And walk out. In order to survive survival, you must first survive.

Victims Seek Justice

The focus on punishment when dealing with victim rights, in my opinion, is a focus on revenge and retribution. While punishment is of utmost importance, it should not be the sole focus in dealing with victim rights and advocacy. It is my experience through life and research that the criminal justice system is out of balance when weighing rights. The victim has rights; yet, so does the offender. In weighing those rights, punishment (whether one calls it justice, retaliation, retribution, or revenge) is doled out. Unfortunately, when the rights of the offender outweigh the rights of the victim, the victim is punished. When the rights of the victim outweigh the rights of the offender, the offender can receive a harsher punishment that is warranted by the crime or an innocent individual is found guilty. A true "justice" system need arise from the rubble that is the current "criminal" justice system.

The link between victimization and justice is too dependent on the politics of justice rather than the science of justice. Victimization was taken out of the hands of the human victim (the recipient of injustice and rights violation) and placed in the hands of the State. As such, cases appear on the docket as "State v. Offender name". The victim's rights and voice become second to that of the State. Symbolically, the State is the victim of record. The perpetual question is, why does the victim have to fight so hard to receive the rights they had before they became victims? The secondary question is why does the offender seem to receive more rights once deemed an offender (or alleged offender) than had before the criminal act?

Trulson in his "Reaction Essay" points out several times the goal of the criminal justice system is to be inclusive of victim rights yet "exclusion is everywhere." Trulson (2005) concludes the criminal justice system is not inclusive of all victims. The system seems to pay particular attention to the victims of street crime and property crime. The worth of victims of personal crimes are not a primary concern. I feel this has something to do with the political atmosphere and trends. I often reference the perception of safety. The public is concerned with feeling safe. Domestic violence is a deeply personal victimization. I find more people blame the victim for staying than they consider the offender's abusive behaviors. Unlike rape, many consider domestic violence (especially intimate partner violence) as entirely within the control of the victim. Thus, the community does not consider domestic violence a threat to public safety. However, gun violence is viewed differently. A gun has several bullets and is reloadable. Thus, a crime by way of gun violence is a threat not only to individuals, but to the community. I set forth that any crime is a threat to public safety. All crimes against another human being are a threat to the safety of all human beings. We must fight for further strides toward public education, advocacy, and victim rights. We must help victims become surviving victims. We must work to prevent the generation after generation of offending and victimization in families and communities. Surviving victims of domestic violence must feel their family, community, and church are a part of their strategic plan to survive survival.

Are You a Victim?

(Source: http://psychcentral.com/lib/2006/understanding-the-effects-of-domestic-violence/)

If you answer yes to any of the questions below, you may be a victim of domestic violence. You may take action and stop abuse by referring to the Guidelines for Victims of Domestic Violence section.

- Are you in a relationship in which you have been physically hurt or threatened by your partner?
- Has your partner ever hurt your pets or destroyed your clothing, objects in your home or something special to you?
- Has your partner ever threatened or abused your children?
- Has your partner ever forced you to have sex when you did not want to or does your partner ever force you to engage in sex that makes you feel uncomfortable?
- Do you ever feel afraid of your partner?
- Has your partner ever prevented you from leaving the house, seeing friends, getting a job or continuing your education?
- Has your partner ever used or threatened to use a weapon against you?
- Does your partner constantly criticize you and call you names?

A Victim Before His Birth?

A t birth, my son "Jordon" seemed perfect. He had a slight cough; so, I asked the nurses if it were possible for babies to be born with a cold. The nurses comforted me by telling me Jordon was perfectly healthy with an Apgar score of nine. This being my second child, the cough still concerned me. I drifted to sleep wondering why. I awoke realizing I was sleeping too long to have just had a baby. With my first son, DaVante', the nurses only allowed me to rest briefly. I could not get a straight answer from the nurse as to why they did not bring my baby boy to me. I adjusted my clothes, and went on a mission to find what happened with my baby. Eventually, I found out Jordon was in NICU. His brain was not telling him to breathe or do anything else. They called it a severe form of apnea. Later, the doctors diagnosed respiratory syncytial virus (RSV).

My sweet baby boy had tubes in this head, throat, arms, and feet. Machines, a ventilator and respirator, were breathing for him. Jordon was so tiny. There were tubes in his little nose, wires connected to him, and IVs in arms, feet, and partially shaven head. It was scary seeing his eyes shut to the world and seemingly his future. I cannot explain the fear and grief I felt each time the hospital told me my son died. God was with him. After three failed attempts to take him off the respirator and ventilator, I received yet another call to come say "goodbye." By the time I got up the almost 5 or 6 city blocks up the hill on foot to the hospital, God gave my son the strength to pull the tubes out himself. From that moment on, his breathing was fine. From time to time, he had bouts with asthma which he later outgrew. I thought the price for the beatings had finally been paid. Jordon was growing and developing well.

I was wrong. Over the years, Jordon grew indifferent to other children. He preferred not to have friends. If he did allow other children around him as "friends," he treated them more like toys or objects than people. He often accused them of plotting against him and hating him. He committed some semi-violent acts that seem unprovoked and unjustified. The instances were few, and far between; so, I did not give it much thought. I just figure he was eccentric.

In November 2007, Jordon began having difficulty in school. He was inconsolable and violent. The elementary school referred him to the local mental health emergency room many times. Each time the hospital released him and cleared him as no danger to himself or others. His first admittance to a hospital child and adolescent psychiatric unit (January 2008) was heartbreaking and horrifying. The school videoed him talking to people who did not exist, running through the school, hiding in closets, accusing school staff of threatening to harm him, and flipping over school furniture. The last straw was when he began to hurt or threaten others (including his brother and friends) claiming the school principal instructed him to do so. When asked "why" he said the voices told him to do so. He admitted to seeing images and hallucinations that other people did not see. He got worse leading to breaks from reality. At one point, Jordon begged me to tell him where his mother went. I felt helpless. How does a mother help a son find the mother in front of him?

However, after many more hospitalizations, Jordon hurting himself, him trying to stab DaVante', holding a knife to a neighbor child, etc., his psychiatrist diagnosed him with schizoaffective disorder. That diagnosis eventually changed. At the time, doctors told me that a diagnosis so severe in children this young (then age 8) it is due to excessive stress and trauma to the mother while she was pregnant. This assessment is supported by some experts and disputed by others. Genetics as a factor is more widely accepted than the preceding theory. While Ivan is not in our lives (after moving 8 times to get away from him), and he does not know about my son's mental health issues, I still have to deal with the abuse daily. I have a mentally ill son at the hand of an abuser. I have a healthy son that has to deal with the abuse and stresses of a mentally ill brother.

Jordon says this of his visual hallucinations, "When I see stuff it can be scary and violent. Like people and things trying to kill or destroy me." At an interview to enroll Jordon is a new school, he looked at the clinician and said, "There is a man in the corner with a knife. He wants me to kill you. But, don't worry I'm not going to kill anybody." Long story short, he was not accepted into that school. His visual hallucinations are quite elaborate at times.

Sitting in the living room one Sunday afternoon, Jordon told his in-home family therapist about a place he goes. He explained that he is taken there, and it is difficult to get out. I listened as he told me of mountains, violent people, cuddly monsters, and rough terrain. I watched as he drew pictures with frustration – he could not draw the images as he saw them. Then he spoke of our park visit the day before. DaVante', Jordon, and I had such a fantastic time, or so I thought. With the therapist, we laughed about Jordon's inability to catch the ball. Jordon hung his head down, let out a deep sad sigh, and described being taken into a world that looked like the park, but somewhere else. He called it "my own little world." That day at the park, Jordon described, the "world" had an exit sign. He told us that as he tried to walk toward it (we thought he was just distracted and exploring the park), the exit sign moved. He whimpered as he remembered feeling trapped, as if the "world was closing in on him." A tear fell as he expressed his fear that he would never see us again. I did not know. I played with my sons in the park that day not knowing that Jordon was experiencing such fear, such torment. I sat feeling inadequate.

As of today, age 12, Jordon is a diagnosed schizophrenic-paranoid type. His doctors worked to rule out other mood disorders. It is devastating to watch him struggle with the reality he knows and the reality others live – they are not one in the same. Recently, Jordon called me from the hospital excited that he had not lost his superpowers despite his recent medication adjustments. Throughout the long hospitalization, four months, Jordon fought with audible and visual hallucinations, delusions, and paranoia. I will never forget getting a call from a nurse telling me that Jordon went into his hospital room and tied a sock around his neck in an attempt to kill himself. His reason, "The doctors and nurses, staff, are trying to kill me. So, I'm going to kill myself. I am not going to let them kill me here. They don't want to help me, fix my meds, they just want to kill me."

The doctors were in the midst of changing his medication, so he was on an extremely low dose that was nowhere near a therapeutic level. I am not sure I was ever so scared, or cried so hard. The thought of losing my baby boy, I just could not bear it. There was no one to hold me up, to comfort me, but God! Later I asked Jordon if he remembered this or similar times. He said, "Sometimes I feel like dying - It is hard to remember my family love me. Everybody has their moments, I guess. I really try to just get through it. It's hard to know if it's me or the people in my head." Again, my heart sank as I refused to let him see the tears fall. I could not help but feel a sense of pride as Jordon and I sat at the table discussing his experiences. Through all of this, he grew up, he matured. Jordon sat up straight expressing his feelings and describing his experiences.

He wants people to know. He needs people to understand. I am such a blessed mother to have him!

Late in 2012, the world turned our attention to the twenty children and six school personnel murdered in Newton, Connecticut. The case, still ongoing as of the writing of this book, caused many to comment on mental illness, mentally ill children, and parenting mentally ill children of any age. I found myself lost in a whirlwind of emotions. Primarily, of course, I was heartbroken for those families who lost children, teachers, family, and friends. I was heartbroken for the town of Newton. I was saddened for children who hoped to one-day graduate together who instead died together, and would be buried around the same time. It was such an inconceivable tragedy.

I, then, found myself fearful. I feared speaking out against the illogical and false information about mental illness overtaking mainstream media and casual conversation. I feared the insensitive comments of others. I feared how others would see my son. Over two years ago, Jordon gave me permission to tell his story. His older brother, DaVante', thought it a necessity. I hesitated. I was scared. My children had greater strength than I. Why? It was clear to me that once I told Jordon's story, my story, it became real. I would never be able to live a day in denial. Even on his good days, his illness was before me. The strong sense of responsibility awakened within me in the days following the Newton shootings. The fear left. Purpose overwhelmed me. Faith engulfed me. Jordon, not knowing about the incident in Newton, asked me when I was going to finish the book. He looked at me as if disappointed. I assured him that I would work on it. I could not tell him that I was not yet as strong as he was.

After dealing with grief and fear, there was the onset of a new reality. My son hears voices. Those voices at time tell him to hurt others and himself. Most of the time, he does not act.

However, as Jordon gets older, he complains that he cannot tell which thoughts are his, the voices, or thoughts that are not his own but with no clear origin. The paranoia was once a minor complication of his illness, now it is the most difficult. He has his way of testing, "I ask people if they are really trying to get me or if they are really teasing me, laughing at me." Unfortunately, at the height of a paranoid episode, Jordon does not always have the conscious ability to use his coping and reality testing skills. He can only exist in the fear.

When discussing the material for this book, Jordon said, "When you hear voices, it is loud and it hurts your head. You cannot stop it! It is in your head and ears." Tears welled up in my eyes, but I refused to let them fall. I was so proud of his transparency. He continued, "For me, the voices sound like regular people sometimes. Sometimes it sounds like there are lots of people talking and screaming at the same time. You know, like a lot of people telling you to do stuff at once." Listening to Jordon as he tried to explain gave me a glimpse into his world. I understood that while paranoia offers the greatest challenge to parenting Jordon, for Jordon the paranoia is the least of his concerns. After all, does he even know whether he is being paranoid? He fears the unreal voices and images.

When asked about how he deals with the voices, Jordon explained, "The good voices are better, but I still try to keep my mind off of it and hope they go away soon. I do try to remember the good stuff. I try. Sometimes the good voices give me advice about [how to deal with] the bad voices." I told him that I would not be able to focus on anything. At that moment, I was no longer a mother. I was a student, and he was my teacher. Jordon instructed, "I focus more on trying to stay occupied and do something to distract me. For example, if I am playing Legos and the voices come than I focus on the Legos so the voices get tired of trying to get me to listen and they either go away or they get mad. Either way they stop if I concentrate hard enough. Well, that's if my meds are working. Today, they are working just ok."

He expresses frustration that sometimes he does not know what is right or wrong. He does not know whether he should act. Furthermore, he cannot determine whether his action will have a positive or negative consequence. When asked about this, Jordon replied, "After I hurt someone, I mostly don't remember it. But, I feel bad and guilty. I feel like they don't want to see me anymore or that they hate me. But, I don't mean to do things to people. The voices take over I guess. I mostly don't remember. Sometimes doctors say it's because I'm paranoid." Jordon said, "I don't always know when I am hearing voices. Sometimes I do bad stuff because I am not sure if the voices are my thoughts or if they are voices. Sometimes I think the voices are real people talking." Thank God, most of the time Jordon's thinking is clear enough to express his concerns and tell his doctors and me when his medications are not effective. Like he said, "It's hard trusting my thoughts sometimes. But, I try to trust myself. I trust my mom and some of my doctors."

One thing people outside of the situation do not understand is the struggle of the parent. It is hard simultaneously being a mother and an advocate for your child. You want to coddle and love them. Unfortunately, since I am in the position of being Jordon's greatest advocate (or worst) it is not always possible to sit back and just be a mom. I have to attend meetings, convince doctors that he insists his psychiatric difficulties are increasing, and endure test after test. There is no guarantee that he will be re-admitted to the same hospital during each crisis or when he needs an emergency medication change or adjustment. With each hospitalization, there is a new set of doctors. Most doctors immediately assume there is something wrong with his home life and that every doctor before them had mis-diagnosed my son. Once they observe him, they are clear about his symptoms. Jordon says this about hospitals: "How it feels to be in a locked facility or hospital - You feel trapped and you have no freedom or rights. It feels like you are locked in a box. But, at the same time, you know you need to be there. It messes up your schedule. The doctors don't understand sometimes."

I used to think calling someone an "advocate" was a compliment. Now, I know that some in the mental health field use this term synonymous with "problem parent" or "difficult parent." I am told that I am the only one who truly knows my son and that they value my input. Yet, when I offer input, sometimes I am treated as an intruder or someone they simply tolerate. It becomes a battle of wills. They know the patient, and I know the child. It takes time and flexibility, but I am grateful for the team of doctors, therapists, and case managers who worked with my son over the years. We did not always agree on my son's path to stability. We did, however, agree that how we personally felt was secondary to his needs. I refuse to stop advocating for my son. I refuse to stop believing God for his healing. I refuse to stop being his mommy!

Aloneness. This journey is the hardest of all I have endured. Trying to maintain DaVante's mental and physical health while catering to the mental health needs and emergencies of Jordon is such a lonely road. There is not a day that has gone by that I felt someone understood. No day where I felt supported. I attend meetings alone. I protect my children alone. I carry the weight of protecting the world from Jordon. After the Newton incident, I felt the general public attacked parents of mentally ill children rather than supported us. The aloneness intensified. The general assumption that we are incapable of protecting our children is flawed. We, I, try our best. I carefully choose where we go. I monitor changes in the environment any place we visit. I keep Jordon away from babies and other unpredictable people. The voices often tell Jordon to remedy loud noises and the unpredictable behaviors of others in highly unorthodox or inappropriate ways. My sons and I have code words to know when it is time to leave a situation without a drawing attention.

I cannot speak for all parents. The parents I know try their best. If our child should hurt himself/herself or someone else, we carry that guilt. I try to remind myself that I am not God. I am human. I can only do but so much. In doing all I can, I only remember missing 2 appointments in the entire length of his illness that was not due to an unavoidable emergency. One of those appointments was because I was just too overwhelmed and exhausted. Another way I do all I can is to make sure he is safe. I guide transitions between hospital, residential treatment facilities, and home to make sure he has the optimal success. I work so hard to make sure the world is safe for and from Jordon.

He is such an incredible boy. I do not regret this journey in the least. For this to be our path, I cannot imagine traveling it with a different set of children than the boys God gave me. On the roughest of days, I remind myself of the doctors who told me that I could not have children. I remind myself of the mothers and fathers who have to utilize In Vitro- Fertilization and adoption in order to have a child. I remind myself that Jordon is a remarkable gift. I vow to protect, nurture, and love my gifts, my boys, with all my heart and all my life. I am not cursed to have a mentally ill son – I am truly blessed. Jordon is more than his illness!

My favorite verse in the Bible is Genesis 1:1a – "In the beginning God created…" The verse speaks of the creation of the universe, earth, and all within in them. As I go through difficult days where I feel alone, this verse reminds me that even before the formation of the world, in the very beginning,

God was there. Before Jordon was born, God was there, in the very beginning. God created me. He created my sons – despite the word of the doctors. God created this path. My comfort is in the knowledge that on this path, we are never alone as long as God is there.

There is so much to my story. "Domestic violence" is much too cute of a phrase for the years of pain I have endured. I am so grateful for God presence in, through, and after it all. His love gives me strength and life. Jordon has an extraordinarily long, complicated, and trying road ahead of him unless his symptomology changes or medical science finds a cure. There is no time for me to feel sorry for my plight. It is my duty, and privilege to support him on his journey. One day, I hope Jordon will be able to tell his own story of strength and triumph. He is such an inspiration for me. He simply refuses to give up. His grades are excellent, and his spirits are high. He finds hope in the midst of the darkest despair. That is an irrefutable blessing.

I asked Jordon if he had any advice for those who deal mental illness such as his, for parents, or anyone who wants to understand. Jordon quickly responded with three points of wisdom. He said, "It's important to take your medicine. Don't play with it. People trust you to take your medicine. Don't trick them and throw it away or hide it. It hurts them, and you only end up in the hospital." I instantly thought, I hope he remembers this himself. See, in the past I found pills hidden in plants, under throw rugs, and other weird places. Some times he thought the medication was a part of some elaborate plot and other times he thought he was well and no longer needed the medication. One time he said the voices threatened to kill him if he continued to take his pills. They accused him, he said, of "trying to get rid of them." So, I pray in the future, Jordon remains mindful of the importance of taking his medication for his health and our stability as a trusting family support.

Tonisha M. Pinckney

Jordon offered another point of wisdom, "It is important to tell people my story so other kids and parents can know that I lived through it, and a lot of other people deal with this, schizophrenia. It's very hard. They can know they are not alone." He sums all of his thoughts in saying, "Other people should know that it is not a horrible thing! It is just something that you have to live thru. The doctors and meds do help you. Keep trying."

Mommy's Reality

I want to be the one thing that's real
To understand the fears you feel
Baby boy can you live by my heartbeat
And understand that with God there is no defeat
Reality is relative

You have shown me so much in a short time
One thing is that reality exists in the mind
What you see is different from what others do
But you see it, feel it, fear it - it's real to you
I pray the two collide
Reality and fallacy abide
Reality is subjective

My son, I am ashamed to know I can't walk with you
Look through your eyes and seeing your view
Hear the voices that command
Yell love louder than their violent demands
I want to be your mommy friend
Giving a hug so all tears will end
Reality is oppressive

Instead, I have faith and I pray
The quieting clarity of mind will be born today
Please look into mommy's eyes and see the truth
Let me look into your eyes and find the real you
I want you to live the life the rest of us see
Instead of being trapped in a den while surfing the seas
Reality is unresponsive

You are the most amazing child
I wish to understand the thought behind the smiles
And protect you from walking into a wall pretending to be a door
Or falling down those stairs posing as a floor
And help you understand laughter is not ridicule
Mommies helping their babies is an unspoken rule
Reality is impressive

A Child Witness or a Victim? (Introduction)

U nlike the previous chapters and the ones to follow, my older son, DaVante' penned the next chapter. It was his choice to submit his perspective on two of the main events in our past, domestic violence and mental illness. Before allowing DaVante' to write, I made sure he understood the gravity of his decision. I had to make sure he did not feel pressured. I could not allow him to do this to please me, to spite his father, or out of pain. I stressed the importance of honesty and integrity.

It was difficult to hear how much he saw at such a young age. Honestly, until I read the chapter, I did not know how much he saw. He told me that he tried to protect me by not talking about it. Through the years, I worked with him to help him forgive his father. I hoped that he had forgiven me for not leaving sooner.

In an interview, Brian Martin, founder of Maker of Memories Foundation, told me, "The idea of ending the cycle of violence can never occur, ever, unless you spend at least an equal amount of time focusing on the children who are in these households. I say that simply because more than three quarters of these children go on to repeat what they learned." That is why I agreed to let my son include his chapter. We have to hear the voice of the children. Mr. Martin continues:

"[Children in violent homes] are fifty times more likely to abuse drugs and alcohol. Six times more likely to commit suicide. There's a really simple reason for all of this. Very simple reason for all of it. This is fact-based, this is not my opinion. There is research that's been available only in the past ten years, and I've spoken with these researchers. Our brains – the human brain forms from [ages] zero to four...Then the rest of it kind of forms after that. It forms in childhood and the brain of a child who grows up in a happy, healthy home – let's call it a home without violence – compared to the brain of a child who grows up in a home with violence, is quite different. The brain develops differently. The brain chemistry is different. The nervous system is different.

We create in ourselves, our brain does, a self-concept, a self-identity, a self-concept. That is a fact-based thing. We all have a self-concept. The self-concept changes. It changes fundamentally who these children are, and it only becomes more pronounced as they get older. Stimuli that hits you and me compared to stimuli that hits someone who has grown up in a home with non-violence, strikes us very differently. What may make someone passionate will make me angry. That's what happens. It's not – this is not a soft argument. It is brain chemistry. It's the way the brain works. If you understand how the brain works – this is only available in the past ten years – if you understand how the brain works, you understand that these children are victims. They did not choose to be put in this home.

...A home where there's violence – you are significantly hampered as it relates to having a fair shot to what this country promises, which is life, liberty, and the pursuit of happiness. Full potential."

It is my duty as a parent of a child witness or victim of intimate partner violence to let my son tell his story if he so chooses. He was there. DaVante's experiences were different from mine. The trauma he experienced, related to Jordon's mental illness, are all his own. I could never tell his story as he can. The interview of Brian Martin provided a excellent opportunity to address the needs of children who lived or are living in violent homes. They are not oblivious. They need our attention and support. Ignoring them promotes the continuation of violence from generation to generation. As you read DaVante's chapter, to follow, I hope you grow more aware of the child's voice and perspective.

A Child Witness or a Victim?
(Written by L. DaVante' Pinckney)

Though my life I have seen and endured many things., I have tried to make since of it all. For instance, it took a long time to understand my brother's illness. I skipped going out with my friends and having them come to my house. As I got older, I realized how much my mother sacrificed for my brother and me. She sacrificed her job and her social life. Somehow, though it all, I still had fun. My mother makes sure I enjoy life.

There is so little I remember about my father, "Ivan." I do remember is the sadness of my mother's face as she struggled to try and be strong. All I remember of my father is pain. I remember my father grabbing my mother, and the worse of all putting his hands on her, hitting her.

There were times that my mother tried to leave. She cried a lot. There was this one time I remember sitting in a room with my brother, and it was loud and noisy from my father yelling and my mother crying, My brother and I could hear my parents yelling and screaming. Jordon, my brother, asked me what was going on. I told him not to leave the room, not to go out there. I protected him. Or, I tried. Jordon started crying because of the noise. My mother yelled for us to stay in the room. My mother's face was so bruised. She was so beaten up. She looked as if she was from a movie. I remember feeling so scared; because, I was not sure if my father was going to come in our room. I was terrified that he was really going to hurt my mother. I was also scared my brother would get hurt because he was younger than me. I tried hard to protect my little brother. But, I was little too.

After my father stopped hitting my mother that day. I remember him looking at me with anger. (Usually, times like this, my father would pick my brother up by his arms and just look at him like with such disgust.) My mother came to hold us. She was crying, bruised, and hurting, but she was trying to make us feel better. She kept saying, "It's ok. Mommy's ok." I was worried. I did not know what was going on, or why he would get so angry. I did not understand what was going on. I remember thinking, "Why is my father doing this?"

I overheard my mother having conversations with my grandmother (my mother's mother) about what was going on in our house. My grandmother talked about ways to try to protect my brother and me. Giving us up was not an option for my mother. I remember we had to live in our car a few times to get away from my father, who kept finding where we moved. We had to move a lot to get away from him. I did not understand then why we stayed in the car, but I understand now.

I remember other times my father grabbed my mother by her arm angrily and hitting for no real reason. I would call for her. I yelled for him to stop! I felt like it was my job to protect my mother. I was little, but I was brave. At the same time, I felt helpless because I was too little to do anything about it.

One Sunday after an incident, my father came to my grandparents' church. They were the pastors. I called out to him, "Daddy. Daddy!" He looked at me without any real expression. He just looked at me and kept walking. My grandparents talked to him in the back of the church. Then, he just left. He did not say anything to me. He just left. That was another time when I just could not understand.

I could not understand why my mom stayed with my father so long. I questioned if that was how life and family were supposed to be. I did not know why we did not leave. Now, I feel like my mother stayed so long because it was dangerous for us to leave. I think she waited until she could try to use the court system and do it properly. If she had left without going through the courts and police, she might have ended up like the women I see one the news who end up dead. They end up dead because they do not make the police aware of the violence while they are alive. Or, it takes so long for the police to figure out why the husband killed the wife because the wife never reports what happened to her. No one knows; so, no one can help her. By going through the court system, if anything does happen to my mother, the police will know that my father could be the reason why it did happen. By her going through the system, she warned the police and courts that he was dangerous. But, my mother raised me not to live in fear, but in awareness. So, while I am aware of how his is, I am not that afraid. God will protect us.

I want to try to forgive him. But, it's hard. People try to tell me that I need to forgive, but I didn't want to forgive. Sometimes, I don't want to forgive my father. My mother tells me that I need to forgive him, but sometime I still have a hard time with it. I just don't understand how someone could act like that. I am still dealing with it today.

Domestic violence splits families apart. Kids like me, who see all the violence, can see that the love is missing. It hurts to see your mother, your family, cry. It saddened me to see my parents or family members did not want to look at each other, or that they did not want to (or could not) even be in the same room with each other. It hurt to see those things. It not only hurt them, it hurt me. I had to watch. There is a lot my mom and I did not include in this book. But, I hope you see that your children can see your pain and sadness. We hurt for you. I'm young, but I honestly care about people, how they feel, and their safety.

At one point, I got angry at the world because it frustrated me to see that everybody around me was happy, or, so it seemed. I did not understand why my friends were happy with life, and I had to deal with these moments in my life without telling anyone besides my mother. Then, I realized that if you have no control over the situation, do not worry about it. If you can have faith that it will work out, that is all you can hope for. Hope and faith work together. Before I knew this, I started to worry about everything. I developed chest pain whenever I was stressed. My mom set up an appointment with a family therapist so we all could get help dealing with my brother's illness and stuff in our past. It was a challenge to deal with all that was going on. Talking it out helped. Praying about it helped.

Whenever my brother, "Jordon," had to go to the hospital, I would I have to think what emotion I should feel. Should I feel sad because [Jordon] is not with me? Or, should if feel happy because he is getting help? By getting help from my mother and her taking the time to help me through it all, I was ok, I am ok.

My brother is strong, sometimes. I cannot imagine how he feels dealing with being schizophrenic. I feel like he will go far in life because he does not let anyone stop him. He keeps trying. He does not care what people think of him, and I find that inspiring. One of the many challenges I face with him is that he sometimes does not understand other people's feelings. Sometimes, that makes it hard to handle the situation. But, because he does try, he makes it up in his own way.

The hardest times are when he does something to hurt me, but he does not know why I am in pain. I feel like people look at him with too much curiosity. They are always trying to figure what is wrong with him. Really, he is just like any other kid, when he has the right help. His illness did not at all ruin my child hood. In fact, we have had some great memories. Like the times when we sat in the hospital, and we would have food and movies while "camp out" with [Jordon]. My mom tried to help us make the best of the situation. There was the time when Jordon was in a hospital for a few months in Maryland. We drove or flew to visit him often. The times when we stayed in Maryland for days or weeks at a time with him, my mother took me to Washington, D.C. to museums and visited other sites along the way. Times like those are a chance to leave the bad situation, and create new memories that were great.

We have had our downtimes, like when Jordon's illness was really bad. It was the first time ever Jordon tried to lunge a knife at me. He was paranoid and accused me of being in the military. After that, he could not recall what had happened. Jordon denied that he did or would do something like that to me or anyone else. I explained to him that I was not in the military; it was just a dream of mine. I did not know he was paranoid, and he took what I said wrong thinking I was actually in the military. I thought my brother could have seriously injured me. It has scared me that day, and ever since. I remember sitting in the house and at the hospital hearing the treatment plans thinking "Wow!" my brother goes through so much. My mother made sure the doctors explained it all to me so I can begin to understand.

Though it all my source of strength came from God and my mom. They have both been there to support me with all by problems. When I was down, they picked me up. I could not imagine going through life without God. My mind could not fathom losing my relationship with God; because without God, I would not have the heart to take such painful experiences.

"I AM MORE" has been applied to my life since the day I was born. "Excellence not excuses" is my motto for school since I started school. This helped me succeed and get A's and B's. My mother did not me stop pushing for my success even though tough times with my brother. She does not let me slip. I wanted to prove not that only am I smart, but that in life, no one will stop me.

My advice: Do not live your life always worrying about what is going to happen next. Instead, make the best of the situation. Do not make excuses for why you cannot do something. There is a time for everything. My favorite scripture is Ecclesiastes 3:1-8 (NIV).

It says:

"There is a time for everything,
and a season for every activity under the heavens:
a time to be born and a time to die,
a time to plant and a time to uproot,
a time to kill and a time to heal,
a time to tear down and a time to build,
a time to weep and a time to laugh,
a time to mourn and a time to dance,
a time to scatter stones and a time to gather them,
a time to embrace and a time to refrain from embracing,
a time to search and a time to give up,
a time to keep and a time to throw away,
a time to tear and a time to mend,
a time to be silent and a time to speak,
a time to love and a time to hate,
a time for war and a time for peace."

This shows that there are times and reasons for not doing things, but it matters how you use them. There is no time for excuses. I struggled with this concept. I made excuses for everything. Life has not been easy, but I made the best of it.

I had to grow up without a father, but to me, my mother filled those shoes. From what I hear, I am becoming a great young man with an active goal. Since I can remember, I have always talked about serving this country. I did not have an idea what branch I wanted to go into until I saw machines that soared though the sky and at such speed. I was mesmerized! I wanted to know everything I could about airplanes. I knew then that I wanted to design and create aircrafts as an engineer and pilot for the United States Air Force (USAF). After a brief time with the Civil Air Patrol, a bunch of visits to air and space museums and shows, and talks with my mother's friend (who is a Major in the USAF), I knew I wanted to change the world. I want to be a part of the process of inventing and improving the best aircrafts to protect and defend the greatest nation in the world, the United States of America. I plan to dedicate me life to protecting and defending my family, friends, and all people of this nation. As my mother says, I survived survival, and I will grow strong. I AM MORE!

Awakened By a Dream
That Was Once a Reality!

O ne night in 2012, while I was sleep I had a dream within a dream. As I dreamed, I realized what I was experiencing was a memory not a dream. I remembered what I went through over a decade prior.

When I woke up one morning in January 2000, I decided I was no longer going to be Ivan's punching bag. I decided, I was no longer going to put up with his cheating on and stealing from me. I refused to deal with the belittling words and demeaning names. Later that morning I took a pregnancy test. I found out I was pregnant with our second child. Knowing I wanted to leave, I hide the pregnancy test deep in the trash. I was in planning mode. I knew I could no longer live through the violence I was living with. If I stayed, I would die.

When Ivan somehow found the pregnancy test, a new level of fear fell on me. He insisted that I walk with our 10-month-old son to the nearest hospital over three miles away for an official pregnancy test. He demanded that I was not to come back home until I had proof from the doctor that I was pregnant. I tried to call people – no one was available. So, I walked.

The tests confirmed that I was pregnant. In tears, I told the doctor I wanted a blood test and needed proof to say I was pregnant. I made up some story – a story I cannot recall – to get him to give me the test results with his signature. Tearfully, I returned home. On that cold day of a new year, I walked home. I walked back to Ivan. I walked back to his fist.

That was a decade ago. I dreamed the memory like it had just happened. I felt every blow against my eyes and my stomach. I felt blood drip from my nose. I heard him spewing out accusations that I planned the pregnancy to trap him because I knew he was leaving. I remembered thinking I did not know he wanted to leave, but knew I needed to leave. I remembered his roses and his apology. His words echoed in my ear once again, "I was just scared because we are so young to be married and trying to have another baby." I replayed my forgiving, yet fearful, tears cooling my skin still burning from the bruising and swelling.

Over the next 3 days and lasting 7 months, he displayed an undeniable determination to punish me for being pregnant. He said and did everything he could do to convince me to abort the heartbeat in my belly. He did everything he could do to punish me for getting pregnant. He did everything he could do to punish me for refusing to "just die."

January 1, 2011, I realized I was still standing. Today, I cannot believe that I endured that. I look in my son's eyes (born later in 2000) with amazement. Through all that, God blessed this world with his presence. I look at that son who was 10 months old in 2000, and I am proud of his focus and strength despite him seeing so many traumas so early in his life. My boys are becoming men – real men!

Our past does awaken us from time to time. The past does fight its way into to our dreams. It is up to us to decide what to do with those memories. We can hold on to them, cry over them, or celebrate our strength. I celebrate the day I finally left (a few years after the incidents described). I will not live full of regret that I did not leave sooner. I know why I did not leave. I forgive myself for seeking and listening to wrong counsel. I forgive myself for thinking I was doing what was best for my children by staying in the marriage. I forgive myself for thinking Ivan's life, feelings, and future were more powerful than my own.

In my dream, I felt fear and relief. I was relieved that I made it out alive. However, I was fearful that he would find us again. That fear did not measure up to anywhere near the fear that another woman might be out there somewhere going through the same or similar set of circumstances.

I am proud that today I can stand and say, "I AM MORE!" I am blessed to look at my children and realize the best thing I ever did for them was saving their mother's life. I am humbled that God took the time to protect me and my unborn child through constant kicks to the stomach, forced to drink rubbing alcohol, and repeated attempts to destroy me during my pregnancy.

"I AM MORE!" is not an empty chant. "I AM MORE!" is a way out. It was when, and only when, I realized "I AM MORE!" and that my children deserved more (because they are "more") that I could walk out of the marriage. I am still careful to protect our home and us. I am still worried about the day he will find us or see us again. However, I know God is a protector of his children. I know that I am still alive so that I can use my voice and story to tell another mother that being a single mother is far better than being a dead mother!

I raise a proverbial glass toasting that dream/memory. I appreciate the reminder that my life has a purpose. I appreciate the reminder that I am to remain cautious. Most importantly, I appreciate God for it just being a dream and not something I am enduring today. I appreciate God allowing me to be a voice of life rather than a voice from the grave. Indeed, "I AM MORE!" Guess what, so are you!

Life After Abuse: You are Important!

W hether classified as the abused or the abuser, there is life after abuse. Unfortunately, one can sabotage their life by not understand that YOU ARE IMPORTANT! Feelings of inadequacy can negatively affect all areas of your life and relationships. Feeling unimportant can lead one to lash out at others or accept abusive treatment from others.

Everyone has a story. Everyone is going through or has been through something. Everyone has to make the same decision – "How do I handle my pain and my stress?" What someone else is going through (or has gone through) does not give them the right to treat you (or anyone else) wrong. The same holds true for you. If you are going through a difficult time, it is not excusable or acceptable for you to treat them badly. You do not have to feel the pain of another person in order to understand their pain. You do not have to inflict pain to get others to understand your pain.

After witnessing a physically abusive episode, my son, DaVante', was shaken and upset. He began to have small panic attacks, and began crying for "no reason." The violent image triggered what we thought were forgotten memories. When he approached an adult aware of the situation, he was told he has to "be in their shoes" and that he has to "understand their problems." This made him feel unimportant. He felt like his feelings and pain did not matter. DaVante' felt like the person talking to him found justification for the violence. Sadly, he felt like the adult did not take into consideration what he had been through (witnessing domestic violence, a seriously ill sibling, sexual bullying at school, and other issues). He felt that adult was more interested in getting him to understand why the person should be excused than helping DaVante' deal with what he experienced. I helped him with his struggle to maintain respect for that adult. He still struggles with whether he could trust that the person responsible for the violence he witnessed. In that instance, DaVante' sought validation. Understanding what someone is going through is not an alternative route to excusing his or her behaviors. Wrong is wrong. You are important! What you are going through is important. His or her pain is no excuse or justification for inflicting pain on you. Many people feel similar to DaVante' did that day. They see what others do, and they accept excuses, rationalizations. They stand in the face of pain feeling empty, without apology. They feel as if their feelings, wants, desires, pain, past, and future dull in comparison to the pain and actions of the person abusing them or those they love.

Points to Remember:

1. An abuser is an abuser! Whether mental, physical, emotional, sexual, spiritual, financial, or psychological – abuse is not justifiable!
2. Understanding their pain does not mean you have to excuse their actions. There is a time for heightened understanding…but the time is not every time.
3. You deserve an apology. Justifying their behavior cheats you out of the apology you need to hear. It also cheats them out of the opportunity to address their actions and receive forgiveness.
4. Do not let anyone tell you to understand the pain of another and ignore your own pain. We all need to understand that everyone is dealing with or has dealt with something. No one's pain is less important than another's is.

5. Everyone is responsible for his or her own actions. If you are not directly involved, push for healing, not just for calm (quiet). Calm is not always peace. Smoothing over the situation could leave life in turmoil.

6. You are important! That is the main thing to understand. Your feelings are important. Your body or mind is not to be abused. Do not allow anyone to step in and justify away (also known as dismiss) how you are feeling.

It is Time to REmind!

L ike you, my mind refuses to forget the pain. Like you, I am guilty of forgetting to remember some of my happiest moments. I know they are there, happy times, but I must coax my mind into remembering for fear that remembering will bring up pains long since forgotten. Like you, I have to remind myself "I AM MORE!"

Some days my mind wanders back to a place that maybe it should not go – to my marriage. Times when I thought I was happy; but not grasping the true meaning of happiness. My mind wanders back to a time when I was hit, spat on, burned with cigarettes, and had Kool-Aid poured over my face while I was in a deep midnight sleep just to see my fight for air. My mind wandered back to the first sexual victimization at age twelve. In those moments, I thought I had survived the worse time of my life. I thought every moment after that would be my happiest. My mind continues to wander to the next rape and the next, to the people who said I deserved what I had endured, to the people who ask what I had done to provoke such vicious attacks.

I remember once I went about a month without Ivan hitting me, cursing at me, or belittling me. I do not remember the date or the time-period. Instead, I do remember the intense sense of loneliness. He and I were laughing, playing with the kids, and making ends meet. He was coming home every night – sober. We were even attending church together. I remember looking in the mirror with tears wondering why things were different. I wondered if he no longer cared, loved me – if he was preparing to leave me. My level of understanding had sunken so low, self-esteem non-existent that I truly felt the lack of abuse equated to lack of love. His cheating, belittling, and violence served as reminders of his love for me. That was how I felt at the time.

I remembered how those (two boys, 3 boys, 1 man, 1 husband) who raped me told me that they did so just because I was there. There was no other reason. They did not say because my looks were enticing. They did not say I did anything to deserve or provoke what happened to me. I could have been anyone. I am so glad another girl did not endure as I did. She may not have been able to endure it. I barely survived myself.

My mind wanders. I remind myself that everyone who told me that I was worthless, that I deserved what happened, that I was without value, was wrong I remind myself "I AM MORE!" I REmind myself that I am loveable and worthy of true love. I had to pray that I experience that love one day. I am no different from you. Some days are harder than others are. Conversely, some days are better than others are. I often say, "A tormentor cannot torment you unless you allow them to do so!" It becomes necessary for me to recondition my mind – REmind – so I can recondition my thinking! You need to do the same.

I push the torment aside and embrace the treasure that is me and within me. I push the beatings aside and embrace belief. I push the pain aside and embrace prayer. Pushing aside does not mean denial. Denial is only delaying pain. Pushing aside clears the path so you can see what is in front of you rather than what happened behind you. Before you can see your future, you must clear a path to it.

I know what it is like to look in the mirror and only see the scars no one else can see. I know too well that moment when you look at your history, and it only tells testimonies of pain and fear. I know what it is like to wonder who will hurt you next because you are not worth anyone loving you more. I also often say, "I survived me!" There is no one who can remind you of who you truly are (well except God and the Holy

Spirit). You have to encourage and remind yourself. When your mind wanders, you have to REmind.

To REmind simply means changing your mind – changing your thinking. It is time to rewire your mind so that your thoughts align with your future, not your past. It is time that you retrain yourself to act based on where you are going not what you went through. It is time you REmind yourself that the negative thoughts you have of yourself are not your own. A person who would work so diligently to plant those thoughts in your life is in some way threatened by your obvious greatness and potential power. REmind yourself!

Saying "I AM MORE!" is saying: I am EXTRA-ordinary. This means I can perform extraordinary feats with ordinary resources. My mind can think up extraordinary ways to accomplish extraordinary successes. My faith, even through my weakest moments, is extraordinary. My extraordinary strength and faith combine with my extraordinary abilities and talents to make extraordinary strides in greatness.

Escaping to the Future

J ust because you cannot move forward (right now), does not stop you from thinking forward (right now). There are obstacles in life. I know this far too well. Often, people ask me how I made it through so much in such a relatively short time – I guess 36 years is a short time. My answer is always straightforward but most often not the same. "It's a journey, so I keep moving." Or, maybe, "God, and nobody but God." My answer is usually whatever comes to mind at the time. My survival had a direct positive correlation to my faith and my thinking, not to what was happening to me. I maintained a forward thinking mentality. Your thinking is your own escape.

Too often, I felt as if life was holding me back. I questioned the reasons my life seemed to be in constant turmoil. Some situations I caused, but most I did not. My circumstances were out of my control, or they seemed. My circumstances grieved me. I reached a point where rapes, abuse by my then husband, someone stealing my identity, a sick child, and a long list of other "stuff" brought me to a mental, physical, emotional, and spiritual stand-still. I did not move. I could not move. Rather, I refused to move. When I reached that point, I soon realized I had to move. I began to think. I thought not about what happened, nor did I think about what I was going through. I made a choice, an active decision, to think about my exit strategy. What could I do to ensure a positive outcome? What could I do while I was at the stand still that would help me move quicker when life again started moving?

Life can be overwhelming at times. That is a fact. We can get so engrossed in family, friends, career, school, and/or organizations that we can feel as though we have lost ourselves somewhere along the line. We look around for an exit. Problem: we do not want to leave our family, friends, career, etc. behind. In most cases, we should not. (Well, some people need to be left behind; but, that is for another book.) We just want to stop feeling overwhelmed.

So what is there to do? Do we neglect responsibilities? No, that will just come back to stress us later. Do we say "no" more often? Could be possible; but, most likely not probable. We like to feel needed while simultaneously we beg for space. Vacations give us a break. When we return, though, we realize that life went on and the number of tasks requiring our attention increased. How do we escape and never leave?

Life is a journey. There must be movement. In order not to feel overwhelmed, we must allow ourselves to move from one thing to another. What is complete must be done. We cannot fully realize our future if we refuse to release our past. Is it possible that you do not actually feel overwhelmed? Is it possible, that you are suffering from the suffocating effects of stagnation? You do need to escape! You need to leave the mental place where you dwelt in fear and torment. You have gotten too comfortable. It is easier to look at the people around you and blame them for keeping you in the same place.

The En Vogue song says, "Free your mind and the rest will follow." This is true. You have the power to break free. You were born with everything you need to advance – everything you need to survive. When you were a baby, no one told you that it was time to crawl or walk. You knew when it was time. No one could hold you back. You soon began to run. No one could catch you. So, then, why are you standing still now? Fight, flight, or freeze. You chose! Your future is your escape. Once you decide to leave the past, live in the present, and have faith in the future, you will escape to mental and emotional freedom. Escaping is not running. Do not run from your responsibilities. Exit the place you are so you can be a more effective resource to and for yourself. So, escape-exit! This is your secret weapon in the fight to survive survival.

I Still Believe!

I have experienced hurt, but I still believe in healing. Hate reared its horrific head in so many ways, yet I still believe in love. Heartache followed pain which followed fear which came immediately before loss, yet I still believe in God. Born to a single mother and once a battered wife, still I believe in family. I waded in the shallow murky waters of fear, yet I dug deep and found hope. I was abused and used by boys and men, and still I believe in the strength, integrity, and purpose of the black man.

It was crucial to me to admit that I still believed. It meant I had to admit that I once believed in all those things and more. Unfortunately, I also had to concede to the fact that I had once lost faith in any one of those things at some point in time. But, at some moment, I stood in the face of all I went through, put on a smile, looked to heaven, and said, "I still believe!"

Hebrews 11:1 says, "Faith is the substance of things hoped for and the evidence of things not seen." By losing hope, I was in danger of losing faith. I never thought I could reach that dark place of hopeless, yet I did. I no longer believed that I would experience the gifts of life. I was not sure if I was worth love, healing, happiness, family, or even God. I grew to realize that God never lost faith in me – He still believed in me!

I got through that set of raindrops by believing God still believed in me. If He believed in me, then who am I not to believe in myself? Who am I not to trust God's assessment of me and my capabilities? Suddenly, I felt revived, though distracted by all that was going on in my life. Expressing and embracing my belief in positive results enabled me to see the situations as temporary and empowered me to hold strong until the end. I could live as long as I still believed.

You may not have yet reached your "I still believe" moment. You may stand staring pain, hopelessness, and despair in the face wondering if that is all that is left to life. I have been there. I thought not living was the only answer to not dying. Okay, so maybe that made no sense. Nevertheless, it was what I thought at the time. You have to want to see something better. You have to want to believe in something. It does not have to be a long list. Just start with one thing, person, and feeling. Just like fear, faith has an astounding ability, to multiply.

You do not have to believe in everything immediately. I wish I could say it started with me saying, "I still believe in God." Even after my near suicide attempt, I remember first believing in me. It was strange. It was the voice of God that rescued me. It was the words, "See how much you are worth," which led me to believe in myself. To this day, I wonder if this meant I never lost faith in God or if it meant that God knew, at that moment, it was more beneficial for me to believe in me. Maybe He knew I still believed in Him, still knew His voice, or still had faith in His power to save. Whatever the reason, I stand here grateful. Whatever reason, you are still here. If you cannot hear God's voice, I hope you will hear mine as I tell you what God told me, "See, how much you are worth!"

When I speak to men, women, boys, and girls, I look in their eyes for the sparkle that tells me that they still believe in something. I pray that if the hope is not there when at first I speak, it will be there with my closing thought or prayer. When I deliver the "I AM MORE!" message in various ways, through an array of topics, my hope is to ignite a spark of belief that burns so intensely it consumes the fear within. Just a spark. A belief that they can, will, and even are surviving survival.

Saying "I AM MORE!" is saying: I believe in me. I will not expect others to believe in me when I have failed to believe in myself. I believe I am successful. I believe I am great. I believe I am powerful. I believe I am intelligent. I believe I am faithful. I believe I am talented. I believe I am resourceful. I believe I am credit-worthy. I believe I am...MORE!

Dear God, For Love

I wrote a prayer, a cry to God, several years ago. After writing it, I found myself in places where I had to speak with others who felt the same way. At the time, I thought I was alone in my feelings. It was a part of my process of surviving survival. It was a part of my healing. This letter to God was my way of purging so I could heal. Revisiting what I said in a previous chapter, I had love but my pain prevented me from feeling that love. I was broken. My numbness to life also numbed me to love.

This letter was actually the beginning stage of feeling. Before I wrote the letter, I am not sure I even realized I could not feel love. I thought I was ready to love and be loved – I was mistaken. The moment I penned this letter, I did – I felt – I prayed – I was ready for love. I knew I did not have love; but, until this moment, I never admitted I needed it. I never admitted the relationship with Ivan was not an example of true love. I had to confess my pain so I can experience love.

I share this prayer with you, not for pity. I do so in the hope that if you are one who felt this pain, you will also see that I survived the pain. It is essential to acknowledge your weakness so you can begin to search for your strength. Acknowledging your weakness allows you to recognize and accept love. It is okay to confess your loneliness. It is okay to be human. It is not a part of your decline, but a sign of your preparation to ascend. You are on your way to surviving survival.

Here is the unedited letter I wrote:

"Dear Lord:

You are my God! I look to you for all that I need and desire. You know what's best for me. I have so much I don't understand. There is so much I just want to happen. So, much I need. Love is the greatest of these. I still don't feel worthy of love. I still don't feel good enough to be loved. I still don't see why anyone would love me. I need to see me through your eyes.

Lord, Father, why do you love me. I know your love is unconditional. I know Your love is not dependent on Who You are not on who I am, was, or will (will not) become. I know I will never deserve Your love. But, I do know You deserve my love. You have my love!

My question is: Do I deserve a man's love? Do I deserve a mother's love? Do I deserve a father's love? A sister's love? A brother's love? These are all the loves it seems like I never can obtain. It hurts more than I can say. It aches more than even I can believe. You are the God of love. You created love! You created me! You created me with so much love to give, yet it feels like You didn't create the love I need. I know my feelings have to be wrong! They just have to be! Why would the God who created me, Who knows me and all about me, Who promised to give me the desires of my heart, Who promised never to leave or forsake me, deny me my greatest desire and His greatest gift – LOVE! Your Word says without love everything we achieve is nothing. The thing missing is LOVE!

I do not ignore the love from my children. I do not ignore the love from the few friends I have in my life. I do not ignore the love my mother tries to give me in her own way.

But, after all I have been through…all the abuse, all the pain, all the rejection, all the injuries, I need a love that tells me none of that matters to him. That I am sexy, attractive, worthy of love, and not damaged goods.

That is what it is...I know I AM MORE! But, I still feel like damaged goods. There doesn't seem to be anything I can do about it. I wish I could give up the desire and wanting to be loved by a man. However, I think if I do give up then I am saying I no longer have faith in You supplying for this need. Only the One Who knows all of your needs can minister to and supply for your every need! You know my need for love. You know how my heart aches and fears that I will die without ever really truly being loved.

I am tired of crying the same tears. I am tired of hurting the same hurt. I release it all to you. I am trusting You even more than I did. I know You can do this.

Oh yeah! That's not all that is bothering me. I need direction. Not just internal direction, but the direction when circumstances shift and make the path clear. Light my path, Oh Lord. Change the direction to Your will. I need guidance. I need mentoring. Wait – I am telling You what I need, but You already know. But, you said ask! So, I am asking! Not demanding, asking.

I need you Lord! I feel my strength is running out! You are my strength in my times of weakness, and I am relying on You. Today I am weak, weakened and weakening. I need love!"

I survived this. You will too! In order to truly survive survival, you must acknowledge your true feelings. Denial is delayed pain! You will not heal if you never admit you are hurt. If you do not admit you are hurting, you will not seek help. Whether you seek help from God, family, friends, mental health professionals, or any combination thereof, the first step is to admit you need healing. I wrote this letter at the precise moment I cut through the denial and confronted my pain. It was a few years after the abusive relationship with Ivan and other unfulfilling relationships. You can write your own letter, say your own prayer, or express yourself in whatever manner is most comfortable for you. The medium of expression is not nearly as important as the act of expressing.

Saying "I AM MORE!" is saying: I am worth it! I am worth the love it takes to love me. I am worth the salary it takes to compensate me. I am worth the hope it takes to have faith in me. I am worth the strength it takes to protect me. I am worth the hug it takes to embrace me. I am worth the words it takes to correct me. I am worth the time it takes to be with me. I AM WORTH IT!

I Am More Concerned

Early in 2012, happy with where my life is heading, I began thinking of my future husband. I did not know who he was or if, for that matter, I have ever met him. While I am single, it is essential for me to prepare my heart and mind to accept his past just as I hope he is preparing his heart and mind to accept mine. Many older women counseled me on the importance of writing a list of all the qualities I want in my future husband. As I sat to write the list, I realized, I did not want to measure a suitor by a stringent list. Which items on the list take precedence over others? What if I dismissed the "perfect" man for me because I did not consider other often hidden qualities? So, I thought about some of the things that may exist in his past. I wrote a poem to communicate my willingness to accept his past, celebrate his present, and co-produce a successful future.

I Am More Concerned

I am more concerned
I am more concerned with your heart than your color
I am more concerned with your vision than your reality
I am more concerned with your love than your sexuality
I am more concerned with your hope than your fears
I am more concerned
I am more concerned with your future than your past
I am more concerned with your honor than your words
I am more concerned with your education than your entertainment
I am more concerned with your legacy than your longevity
I am more concerned
I am more concerned with your peace than your possessions
I am more concerned with your purpose than your plan
I am more concerned with your vision than your sight

I am more concerned with your power than your privilege
I am more concerned
I am more concerned with your freedom than your bondage
I am more concerned your heartbeat than your heartbreak
I am more concerned with your greatness than your lack
I am more concerned with your assets than your liabilities
I am more concerned
I am more concerned with you than what others say about you
I am more concerned with you than what others did to you
I am more concerned with you than what others took from you
I am more concerned with you than what others told you
I am concerned...not worried!

"I LOVE him/her because he/she MAKES me happy!"

A relationship is a bond. However, you should not feel as though you are in bondage! Can love survive survival when measured by level of happiness?

In listening to many people, I hear a constant complaint. "He/She doesn't make me happy anymore!" I also hear, "I am looking for someone who will make me happy!" It is as if love is a by-product of happiness. Almost as if saying, "I love you for making me happy." This type of person measures love by the amount of happiness produced by the relationship.

Am I the only one who sees the selfishness in this way of thinking? "HE/SHE doesn't MAKE ME happy anymore!" "I am looking for someone who will MAKE ME happy!" Some are the first to say, "No-one one but God [and the IRS] can make me do anything!" Happiness is a personal emotion. No one can make you happy!(In my understanding, God offers you joy, but it is up to you to embrace it.) Happiness is dependent more on superficial circumstances than that of joy. Joy is available and possible in the midst of the unhappiest events in life. Ultimately, it is up to you to be happy.

A MATE CAN ONLY ADD TO YOUR HAPPINESS. HE OR SHE CANNOT MAKE YOU HAPPY!

Yes, adding to one's happiness is a monumental responsibility. To add to the happiness of another is also a responsibility that one can realistically fulfill. MAKING someone happy is impossible, and to try could be detrimental. Think of the outcomes. What happens when that significant other expends all of their energy to make you happy, and the very things they are doing decreases their happiness. What about when that man or woman does not understand (or even have) what it takes to MAKE you happy? Even worse, what happens when YOU do not know what it takes to MAKE you happy OR what it takes seems to change as often as time on the clock? Only you can make yourself happy. Only you can allow yourself to be happy.

If you are not happy (in general) as an individual, should you embark on a relationship?

Are you ending a potentially great relationship because you are not in a personal place to feel and achieve happiness and not because your significant other is incapable of making you happy?

It is acceptable to say, "I am most happy when I am with my wife/husband or boyfriend/girlfriend." "I know a new level of happiness when I am with him/her." Phrases like these say two thing: (1) I am already happy. (2) I understand it is not my significant other's responsibility to make me happy. The great thing about reaching this level of understanding concerning happiness is you also realize YOU cannot MAKE him or her happy. They must also be happy. Take the pressure off yourself. Share in your significant other's happiness. Allow him or her to share in your happiness. Add to the happiness of one another. Again, a relationship is a bond. However, you should not feel as though you are in bondage!

If your love is based on someone MAKING you happy, then expect love to be temporary and be ready for heartbreak.

Remember to love your significant other for who they are and who God has predestined them to become. The feeling you get when you are in their presence is a factor when your heart decides to fall in love. How you continue to feel as days turn into decades is an essential element to staying in love. How you feel about your significant other is most valuable to answering the question of love. Love yourself and be happy with yourself. Look to your significant other to add to your happiness and watch the love grow.

In order for your love to survive survival, you must be willing to say, "I am the only one who can make me happy. I will not put unreasonable expectations about my happiness on others. I am happy because I am happy, and I will share that happiness. I will look to and allow my significant other to add to my happiness. I will add to his/her happiness!"

Is it really coincidence?

The smallest tasks can teach some of the grandest lessons. One day, I was sitting playing a game on my phone. Winning the game, I was proud of being on my way to a new high score. In the middle of playing, I remembered I planned a SHORT break, not the excessive time the game absorbed. My aim to stay on schedule was in jeopardy. I did not necessarily want to end the game or even pause it. I went on to the next level in the game passing it with only two seconds to spare. I was doing so well. I made it to the next level. That is where I lost miserably. No high score, game over. My thought, "Well at least I can get back to work."

Immediately after, I began to wonder if losing the game was a coincidence. Did I fool myself? I thought I wanted to continue playing the game, but could it be that, in fact, I wanted the game to end. Maybe I could not admit that I wanted it to be over. My mind, subconscious self, knew that it was time to move on to the next task. Had I sabotaged the game so that I could get back to work? Was it a coincidence? Can I blame lack of concentration?

How many times has this happened before? My thoughts took me to times during and after relationships that eventually failed. I revisited jobs and businesses that came to an abrupt end at just the right times. Was it God removing me from the situations? Was fate or destiny at the helm? Or, did my mind end the "game" making it easier for me to move on to the next task? I tried to dismiss the course of thinking. "It was a game. Everything is not a lesson." I believe this was a perfect, non-threatening lesson. I cannot say whether I have ended any "games" while on my journey. I can say I will be attentive going forward. I will pay attention to situations in the future. I will not be so narrow-minded to think that everything is a pure coincidence.

Yes, I believe in coincidences. I also believe everything happens for a reason. There is a reason for every coincidence. What role did you play in the "coincidences" in your life? Were there any "games" that coincidentally ended abruptly at a time when you wanted to move on? In other words, did your mind say "game over" while you were still in the midst of a play? We often see this during the last two minutes of a sports game (basketball/football). Whether a team is winning or losing, someone wants the game to be over. In those final moments, the player has to contend with pride, fear, and exhaustion. In those moments, as the final buzzer approaches, one makes decisions based on their heart, their instinct. Only they will know if their mindset is "this game is over."

It is all right to end a relationship, change jobs/careers, relocate, etc. because you are ready for the next task or phase in life. Be careful that you do not mentally sabotage the game (aspects of your life) leaving you with no other recourse but to move on. Make conscious decisions. Connect your mindset to your decision. If a coincidence occurs, assess your role. Could it be that this was an outcome you desired? Save yourself from unnecessary heartbreak and victimization. Play the game out or end the game with pride and dignity. Do not quit before the game is over and blame it on coincidence.

A step to survival: Check your Mirrors!

"Your survival is proof of your ability to survive." I say this to people repeatedly. Sometimes phrased differently, but the message is the same. When we go through life's most difficult moments, we tend to over-focus on the present. Too often we focus more on where we stand than where intend to land. We forget from where we come thus losing sight of where we are going. The future is not behind you.

The past is an excellent point of reference. "Don't live life looking in the rear-view mirror." I am not sure I can hold to this thought as it is. We cannot stare in the rear-view mirror. Nevertheless, we need that mirror. That is why it is there. When we glance at the rear-view mirror, we can see how far we have come and how fast. It gives us a better sense of our proximity to our future goals. More importantly, glancing in that mirror allows us to see what we have already endured. We survived life's traffic jams, bumps in the road, near collisions, flat tires, detours, and even a few roads without challenges. If we do not glance in our rear-view from time to time, how can we cling to our ability to survive?

Over the years, I had to take a few glances in the rear-view mirror. I had to remind myself that my survival is proof enough that I can survive the challenges before me. I had to remind myself that God's love for me in the past was proof enough that He still loves me. For me, it is impossible to omit God in my survival plan.

At some points in my life, I spent a lot of time glancing. I had to pull to the side of the road (on my journey of life), actually look, and stare into the rear-view mirror. I was careful not to stare so long that I relived the pain, but I spent enough time in that mirror so I could remember the strength and the triumph.

Before I could continue to drive forward in life, I had to assess my proximity to my past and my future. I had to check all of my mirrors. What from my past was creeping up behind me? Was there someone in my blind spot? The front windshield is large for a reason. There is more to see ahead than there is to concentrate on in the rear. As I sat on the side of my life's road, I realized I had to check my mirrors and make a few adjustments. My mirrors were positioned to show me things I did not need to see right now. I could see everyone else's triumphs – overlooking my own. I could see everyone else's pains – ignoring my own. I could see my obstacles – minimizing my strength. I had to adjust my mirrors!

The circumstances have not changed. Some may have even worsened. However, my hopefulness has grown exponentially. The best way to avoid seasons of depression is to be proactive. I actively decided to adjust my mirrors to see my ability to survive. I turned my sights away from the negativity of others. I looked beyond my own fears.

Job (the man from the Bible) had those around him suggesting he just curse God and die. As did I. Well, those in my life did not use those words to me directly. Those around me simply showed me the blissful possibilities of turning my heart from God. I read a friend's Facebook post talking about a girl who was contemplating suicide. It reminded me of a place in life I once stood. I immediate asked her to call me.

In telling my story, I was able to look in my rear-view. I was able to relive and revive my strength. My own strength gave me strength. In that conversation, I told her about my outlook on God and faith. Job had an extraordinary faith in God. I, then, brought her attention to the part of Job's story I felt so many overlook. God had a lot of faith in Job. God allowed Satan to attack him in every way without taking his life. God knew that Job would not turn his back on Him. God had faith in Job that no matter the obstacle, Job could survival mentally, physically, and spiritually. I felt that faith. I felt God had similar faith in me. When asked how I survived so much, I used to say, "It's a journey. I just keep going." Through my faith, I began to add, "I survived because I know God has faith that I can survive." Your spirituality aside, you are a survivor. Correction: You are a surviving survivor!

Challenge: Adjust your mirrors, so they reveal what you need to see. Filter out the negativity of others. Pull to the side of the road and check the GPS directions transmitted by your heart.

You are More Successful than You Think

Y ou are only as successful as you think, you believe. When you look at your life, and you see a long line of mistakes, bad decisions, failed relationships, and a sea of tears, it is easy to think yourself to be a failure. It is easier to deny yourself the title of "successful." How do you survive survival when you filed away almost everything you know of yourself in a folder labeled "less"?

1. Redefine the word success! Success is specific to the person. Unlike businesses, which measure success in terms of customer satisfaction, bottom-line, expansion, and such, people can choose what perimeters they will use to determine whether they are living a successful life. These perimeters are unique to the path the person took in life. Success is not defined or measured in terms of the successes or failures of others.

2. Figure out why success is or is not important to you. Some people do not consider whether they are successful. They just live their lives. Happiness is far more important and easier to measure than success. Figure out whether your success is crucial to prove something to yourself or to others. Do you need to be successful just to prove to others that you are not a failure?

3. Realize success is a process. Since success is a process, it requires progress. As one progresses, one will reach various levels of success on the way to being a success. Understand you are a success in process and in progress.

4. Do not confuse achievement with success. Achievement is a form of success. However, if one is to measure

success solely on one's ability to achieve, that person would get extremely weary working to achieve one thing after another. Then forced to question what qualifies as an achievement.

5. Success is not a destination. You do not arrive at success. Each level of success empowers you to achieve the next level of success. You can have as many ticks on your success timeline as you want. Waking up every day is a success. Not smoking that cigarette, taking care of your children, paying your bills – all are successes

6. Failure to another could be a success to you. For example, some may put not graduating college in the failure column of their life. However, maybe you chose the military or to start a business. The route you chose was an alternate path to success. For you, not graduating college may have been a truly wise decision based on your skills, goals, desires, or life purpose. Just because you did not do what others say you should do in order to achieve success, does not mean you are a failure. Measure your success by accessing how your decisions align with your dreams, responsibilities, and purpose. Remember, some do all the "right" things and still fail to achieve their dreams or realize their purpose.

You are only as successful as you think. You are ONLY as successful as YOU think. YOU are ONLY as SUCCESSFUL as YOU THINK! You are what you think you are. You are a success in process and in progress. If you think less of yourself, then you might as well expect less of yourself. If you think more of yourself, then you can expect more of yourself. Do not label yourself a failure because you fear success or the expectations attached to success.

Succeed on your terms. Why work so hard to please people (past or present) who wrote you off as a failure? Succeed because success is your birthright. Succeed because success is the legacy you want to leave.

Accomplished Awareness

You may look at me and see all the pain – "BUT, I MADE IT!"
I may look aged and worn – "BUT, I MADE IT!"
I may have gained or lost too much weight – "BUT, I MADE IT!"
I may not smile at the same things that made me smile before –
"BUT, I MADE IT!"
Life did not take the path I preferred or chose – "BUT, I
MADE IT!"

My children may not have the mother or father I hoped for
them – "BUT, I MADE IT!"
My financial situation may be unstable or concerning – "BUT,
I MADE IT!"
People may talk about what I should have or could have been –
"BUT, I MADE IT!"
Who I am may be an embarrassment to some – "BUT, I
MADE IT!"
I may not be where I thought I would be by now – "BUT, I
MADE IT!"

I still cry when I think of all I have gone through – "BUT, I
MADE IT!"
I may have lost some friends along the way – "BUT, I MADE
IT!"
My cries for help may at times have drowned out my laughter –
"BUT, I MADE IT!"
I may have felt hopeless and alone – "BUT, I MADE IT!"

I may have been broken more than I was strong – "BUT, I MADE IT!"

If you must define my future by my past – "Remember, I MADE IT!"
If you must remind me of all my prior shortcomings – "Remember, I MADE IT!"
If you must tell the world of all my mistakes – "Remember, I MADE IT!"
If you must refuse forgiveness – "Remember, I MADE IT!"
If you must look past who I am to see who I was – "Remember, I MADE IT!"

Once my tears cleanse rather than sting, I will say – "TODAY, I MADE IT!"
Once my heart understands its power, I will say – "I WILL MAKE IT!"
Once my fear returns to faith, I will say – "I AM MAKING IT!"
Once I realize I am no longer a product of my past, I will say – "YET, I MADE IT!"
Once I accept that I am a facilitator of my future, I will say–
	"I MADE IT, SO I KNOW I CAN MAKE IT!

Excellence Not Excuses!

B efore I explain the concept and importance of "excellence not excuses," I must define the terms. This mantra, alongside "I AM MORE," is very crucial to my daily life. I fight with procrastination. I am not lazy by any means. But, when the issues of life rain on me, I sometimes want to focus more on what I want to do rather than what I need to do. In those moments, I REmind myself, "Yes, I AM MORE!" Then, I question whether my decisions and actions are grounded in excellence or excuses.

Excellence is doing what is right, in the right manner, at the right time, for the right reason, with the right attitude, in a way that will produce the greatest positive impact. A reason, for the sake of this concept, is simply a statement of your circumstance. An excuse is a blockage (situation, character flaw, lack) you allow to prevent you from overcoming a circumstance.

If you are using what you are going through as an excuse, then you are not using it as a testimony! If you are using your past as an excuse, then you are not using it as a resource. If you are using what people have said to or about you as an excuse, then you are not using it as motivation. Lastly, if you are using where you were born and the neighborhood where you live or grew up as an excuse, then you are not using it as a stepping-stone to your future. Successful individuals are those who refuse to live a life based on excuses. They live, create, deliver, and recreate in excellence. Excellence is part of you. One cannot argue with or deny true excellence.

You are the facilitator of your own future. It is your determination to excel in excellence that will differentiate you for others. Being from a single mother home, your decision – excuse or excellence. Growing up in the "ghetto," it is your choice – excuse or excellence. Having a learning disability, you make the choice – excuse or excellence. If you are dealing with long-term unemployment, you have to decide before your next interview whether you will approach the potential employer with excuses or excellence. You are in control of what you present and how you present yourself. Remember, everyone has a past. Everyone has a disadvantage in some way. Use the past positively or become oppressed by it.

My personal motto, and the motto of my company I AM MORE, LLC. is, "You are no longer a product of your past; you are a facilitator of your future." Transform your thinking and you will transform your life. Transform your life now and you will transform your future. Stop limiting yourself to being a result (a product). It is time you acknowledge and define yourself as a facilitator (one who advances forward, makes easier).

The decision to live a life of excellence is not an easy one. It requires facilitation, proactivity. Excellence is not as straightforward as doing what is right. Again, excellence is doing what is right, in the right manner, at the right time, for the right reason, with the right attitude, in a way that will produce the *greatest positive impact*. Operating in excellence does not mean we will not make mistakes. Excellence does mitigate the likelihood of poor decisions and overly emotional responses. The definition provided enables you to think strategically through your decision-making process. It is a roadmap of sorts.

Excellence is freeing. Too many of us fall short (also known as fail) because we are striving for perfection. You may miss that deadline because you are trying to give the perfect work product. You may not appreciate your significant other because you want the perfect spouse or relationship. You set the bar too high. Is that spouse, are you, contributing excellence in the relationship? Unlike perfection, excellence is achievable on the path to success.

My secondary motto is, "Strive for excellence. Trust God for perfection." Only God is perfect. It is my belief that God is the only One Who can deliver a perfect work product. Only He can continue to perfect our relationships and life. Only God can achieve perfection. So, He does not require perfection from us. He will perfect us. He does require excellence. Free yourself from the burden of perfection. You are setting the bar too high for yourself and others. Perfection can cause you to over-look your accomplishments. Perfection can also act as another form of procrastination. Excellence is your key to freedom from the burden of perfection.

People want to know, "What sets you apart from those before you or those after you?" In other words, they want your profile information. A boss, teacher/professor, bank lender, talent agent, sporting coach, etcetera all want to know why you are different. Why should they hire you, admit you into their college, allow you on their team, or invest in your dream? The answer should have something to do with the word "excellence." Yes, you will reach certain obstacles directly connected to your race, class, religion, sexuality, and so on. Those obstacles may at times make it more difficult for you to achieve the success you desire. But, "more difficult" does not mean "impossible" or even "improbable."

Do not allow your reasons to fail (not succeed) to become excuses for failure (not succeeding). Reasons are external. Excuses are internal. Excuses are tourniquets that slow the flow of blessings, success, progress, creativity, prosperity, and legacy. Excuses kill dreams. Excellence nourishes, promotes, and produces visions and dreams activating them in reality. You alone make the choice for surviving survival. It is up to you to declare, "Excellence not Excuses!"

Look Behind the Mask

People are hurting. How do you know this? Well, you are probably one of them. If you have ever been hurt, then do not find it far-fetched that someone else is hurting. Just like physical pain, mental and emotional pain cannot always be seen. The abused wife or husband who wears long sleeves in the summer to hide the bruises, the teenager addicted to pornography to cover the pain of sexual abuse, the man clinging to alcohol to hide the pain lingering from seeing the traumas of war – they are all hurting. The young girl whose tender face lies deep below layers of make-up, that teacher who yells at his/her students without cause, the one who has it all together but sobs quietly in the car on the way to and from work or church – they are all hurting.

Do not get distracted by what you see. Remember it is not about what you see but whom you see. Look past the addiction, the provocative attire and makeup, the anger, or the lovely clothes and jewelry. Take time to get to know the people in your life – the people who cross your path. Are you missing the opportunity to save a life? Are you so consumed by what you see that you overlook the person?

Suicide is real! Addiction is real! Pain is real! Feeling lonely and forgotten is real! Many people are walking around aching on the inside because they feel unseen or overlooked. They feel no one genuinely cares about their wellbeing. Yes, they hold some responsibility. They are the ones who are hiding the truth – right? They are the ones "faking it" – right? Look behind the mask. Why are they faking it? Society tells us that we are to look good at all times. We are taught early in life to "never let 'em see you sweat.: Social norms make it acceptable for us to wear symbols of emotional wealth when, in fact, we are emotionally impoverished.

Who would dare look behind the mask of "I got it all together" covering the pain of the person sitting next to them in church, their cubicle mate at work, or the student or teacher in the class next door? Do you dare look behind the mask of the mother, father, or child sitting in the room wishing they could disappear without dying? Are you willing to use your pain as a GPS leading to the place of someone else's pain? Or, is that person you?

If you are that person, sitting in the dark, wondering why life is how it has been – remove the mask. Find someone, anyone, who will allow you to be yourself. Find someone who will let you cry on their shoulder. It is easier said than done. Once done, it gets easier. It is up to you to choose life. It is up to you to say "I will not give up. This cannot last forever." Choose not to "bail out" before you have the benefit of seeing your victory. You have gone through so much; you deserve to see the moment when you officially win. You deserve to be able to tell people "I MADE IT! You thought I could not, but I did!" That moment is your right. Death cheats you out of that moment. Choosing death ensures your story will end with pain. Suicide takes away your chance for a happy ending. People and circumstances have cheated you out of moments (days, weeks, or years) of happiness. Do not cheat yourself. You deserve to write your story – do not let the person or people who hurt you win. You are strong enough. You made it through yesterday and you made it to the point of reading this post. You must keep making it. Every moment you live, you are living through it, eventually out of it, and past it.

It is time to live! It is time to live life abundantly! It is time to write your future. Every step into your future you are changing your past. How? Well, your future will one day be your past. What has happened to you is not all that will happen. The good in your future will one day be a part of your past. That good you must see. That is your destiny!

If it is not you facing the choice of choosing life or death, look behind the mask of another. See past the nice clothing and see the mother who cannot feed her children. See that she hand washes her clothes so that they do not fade. See past the father who is always there for his children. See that the mother is not doing what she is supposed to do. See his hurt as a single father or struggling husband.

Somewhere there is a girl or boy cutting their flesh to tackle life pain for pain. Somewhere there is a mother laying in the fetal position hurting too badly to cry over the hospitalization of her youngest child. Somewhere, there is a man hitting his wife or children; because, life beat him beyond the point of personal recognition. Look behind the mask of judgment and help!

Everywhere God is there! For everyone, God is there! Through every pain, God is there! God gave us one another to help each other through tough times! Where are you when your brother or sister needs you? It is time to stand and collectively say "I AM MORE," helping one another survive survival!

Living a Life of Transparency

M ost often, we link transparency with revealing parts of ourselves to others. There are other forms of transparency. Take, for example, the truest form, the ability to see through this or that. Living a life of transparency is simply living your life with the ability to see through the present circumstances and situations of the present to the possibilities of the future. Do not find yourself blinded by what is currently happening in your life. If it lies before you thick and opaque, you cannot see what could be. All you will see is what is – what exists.

Your eyes will only see what you allow them to see and what is available to be seen. If you stare blankly at the now, all the obstacles and walls placed before you, as if that is all that exists, all your eyes will see are dead-ends and despair. Conversely, living a life of transparency sends a message from your heart, brain, and soul telling you to see through, beyond, the present. There is a future. Once you see, you can plan, act, and respond appropriately. You will then be able to focus in on the life beyond the problems you currently face. You will be able to focus on making sure your goals and desires become a reality in your future.

Living a life of transparency goes beyond believing, beyond visualization, to the essence of strategic thinking. In order to develop a viable strategy for your life, to survive survival, you must be able to see beyond where you are now. You must be able to develop a plan based on what you can see in the future. No, you do not have to be a fortune-teller or a prophet. Refuse to allow your current condition to block your insight and foresight concerning your future. Focus less on hindsight and more on foresight!

Your present can serve as a blindfold blocking out all sight of your future. You have an option to change the present into a tool to give you wisdom, insight, and practical experience needed to ensure that mistakes of the past do not repeat themselves (meaning you do not repeat them).

The Responsibility of the African-American Dream

As an African-American, Black, woman, writing this book without including a section on the challenges and responsibilities of being an African-American in America would be irresponsible. Conversations within the African-American community often include discussions about the American Dream, Dr. Martin Luther King, Jr.'s "I Have a Dream" speech, and the balance between acceptance and responsibility. I had my share of racial challenges. In speaking with African-Americans of varying socio-economic and educational status about race relations in America, I found a wide spectrum of opinions regarding the existence of prejudice and limitations of race. One common thread, I found, is the necessity for an increased and unified sense of social responsibility within the African-American community. Have we stopped dreaming? Should we stop dreaming? When is the time to awaken from the dream and act?

Dreams are the pregnant women from which our visions and later our new realities are birthed. Dr. Martin Luther King, Jr. eloquently spoke of his dream. He spoke of the dream he had for his children, for this nation. Unfortunately, just like Joseph in the Bible, his life met tragedy when Dr. King shared his vision with the world. He was free to dream. He dreamed of freedom. Dr. King said, "If physical death is the price that I must pay to free my white brothers and sisters from a permanent death of the spirit, then nothing can be more redemptive." His dream was to free the people of this nation (of every color, race, and creed) from the ever-expanding prison of hatred.

Dr. King's dream was not limited to what he desired for his children and other African-Americans in this country. He desired the liberation of the groups of White Americans enslaved by bigotry, prejudice, and unhealthy bias. That desire existed with the acknowledgement that not all White Americans were working in the spirit of hatred, the majority are not.

Recitation of the pledge of allegiance echoes throughout every school, sporting, and government event in the United States. "I pledge allegiance to the flag of the United States of America and to the republic for which it stands, one nation under God, indivisible, with liberty and justice for all." Dr. King dreamt of the day when every American (Black, White, Latino, or other) could put their hand over their heart and not recite a lie. In my interpretation, Dr. King's dream was that America would one day be comprised of truly UNITED states made up of a united people. I believe, he prayed for us as a nation to stand together under God, His love, and His laws. Dr. King envisioned a country that would no longer allow issues of prejudice and hatred to divide us, but that we would stand indivisible as a show of strength, progress, and power to the world. Furthermore, Dr. King had a dream that freedom and justice would be truly for and apply to ALL in equal measure.

Today, we have an African-American (Black) president, President Barack H. Obama. Some say today's America is the realization of Dr. King's dream. I strongly disagree. Portions of his dream did become a reality. There must still be a fight. The struggle still exists. Today, along with fighting to expand our freedoms and squash injustices, we must fight against our own complacency. We must not accept the freedoms granted as the only freedoms available. Prejudice and racism are alive and well. (We must not forget to include in discussions the prejudices that exist within our own communities.) Alone they are detrimental to the advancement of any people. They become devastating when combined with the complacency of that same group of people. Hope exists when complacency is unacceptable and when courage counteracts fear. Live life moment by moment, movement by movement. There is no standing still. If one is not moving forward, then one is most definitely moving backward. Complacency is nothing more than indifference. Complacency is a refusal to move forward.

As long as we (as African-Americans) continue to blame the "man" for our plight, the dream has not been realized. As long as we, as a Nation, deny the existence of prejudice, racism, and bigotry and the impact of such negative human emotions are ignored, the dream will not be realized. We as African-Americans will not fully realize Dr. King's dream until we fully participate in what it will take to make the dream a reality. We must take responsibility!

His dream was not solely about buying power and executive-level job placement. His dream was about the increased quality of our lives. We are in a better place than ever. However, do not become complacent. Do not think that socio-economic improvement means we are where we could have been or where we should be. I refuse to let my reason for failure, or stagnancy, to become an excuse to fail, or remain stagnant.

I am interested in and passionate about the unjust aspects of the juvenile justice system and the lack of real criminal behavior modification within the criminal justice system. By researching the disparities and advocating for policy change, I consider myself determined to bring us closer to the full realization of Dr. King's dream. As a mother of two young sons, I am training my children to live up to their greatest level of greatness, produce and recognize excellence, and obey the law while working to create change.

What I believe Dr. King wanted for his children was not something that would happen on its own. Equality is the result of just the right amount of pulls and tugs – giving and resisting. Dream your own dream! It is your dream that may be the key to all of us seeing the full realization of Dr. King's dream. Dr. King had a dream. You need to have a dream. You need to pass on a legacy so your children can have a dream of their own!

People may see your color, sexuality, gender, religious attire, and/or ethnic features before they have an opportunity to see you. Make sure, when people see you, the complete you, they walk away with a positive impression. You should be a virtuous person who can stand proud, as did Dr. King and say judge me "by the content of my character." Many cannot make that request because they know their character is not one that should be placed in the forefront. They need to hide behind their looks and any excuses attached. Some people's character cannot withstand scrutiny; they would be left ashamed and embarrassed.

Concentrate more on facilitating your future (your dream) than on those trying to hinder it. Focus more on moving forward than whether others are trying to hold you back. Refuse to be held hostage by the negative character flaws of others (prejudice, misconceptions, and stereotypical responses) and find freedom in the strength of your own character. Dr. King lived and died to see the realization of his dream. You must do the same for your dream. You must pass on a legacy of strong character and virtuous living to your children so they too can live toward the realization of their dreams! Awareness should liberate you! Dreaming is not a privilege; it is a responsibility!

Saying "I AM MORE!" is saying: I will dream. I will know when it is time to awaken from the dream. I will actively make the dream a reality. I will use my reality to invest in the dreams of another.

The Power of Nothing!

My voice called out to you, begging
Your ears heard the intensity in every vibrating syllable
Yet you did nothing
You looked in my eyes, gave me a smile
And did nothing

I am not the forgotten,
I am the ignored
You saw me in need of empowerment
You saw I was undereducated
Yet you did nothing

I could see the lack of concern in your eyes
I could hear your dismissive words
I asked for nothing
You gave me a firm handshake and a promise to return
You have me a fleeting moment of hope

I chased you down as if you were my last chance
I peeped behind every corner of every dead-end
You continued to hide your talent in the highest places
Places I could not reach without your help
You did nothing

Like everyone before you,
I was left disappointed
The next step was unknown
So, I did nothing
You glanced over giving me a smile

I leapt up and ran to you
You smiled again
Realizing I was not the recipient
I turned and once again did nothing
You, seeing my dismay, did nothing

Two roads of nothingness converging
Productivity wasted
Intelligence set aside
I did nothing
You did nothing

We are the same!

Call to Action: Resources for Active Awareness

As individuals, a race, and a nation, we must survive survival! There are a few books I consider a call to action, a summoning to social responsibility. I wrote articles on the books in the past. However, my book would be incomplete were I not to include these resources. Active awareness is necessary. Awareness, while it is vital, is not enough. One must be actively aware. It is time to awaken, to act.

Not in Our Lifetimes: The Future of Black Politics By Michael C. Dawson

It is undeniable that the election of President Barack Obama in 2008 forever changed the political landscape for blacks in America and American politics as a whole. The historical election also revealed an extraordinarily wide divide in the political and economic needs of the black demographic in contrast to white Americans. There is a new wave of political awareness in black communities. From this new awareness rose the question: Is racism diminishing, the same, or on the rise in America?

Michael C. Dawson is the John D. MacArthur Professor of Political Science at the University of Chicago and the founding and current Director of the Center for the Study of Race, Politics, and Culture at the university. His previous books include Black Visions and Behind the Mule: Race, Class, and African American Politics. In his most recent book, Not in Our Lifetimes: The Future of Black Politics, Dawson brings to light the post-Hurricane Katrina and post-2008 presidential election racial climate.

Dawson said during our interview, "The period between the aftermath of Hurricane Katrina and the election of President Obama represents one of the most volatile periods in African-American political history which were marked by extremely rapid changes in public opinion." The public opinion of whites in America, according to Dawson, is quite different from that of blacks. In the book (p. 86), Dawson provides the following statistics: "Ninety-three percent [of blacks] believe that racism remains a problem in the United States...Ninety-eight percent still believe that racism plagues the nation."

The mention of the term "black politics" invokes images of the 1960's marches and the "militancy" of the early 1970's. Instead, "black politics today falls short of having the ability to deliver on the promise of 'no justice, no peace'", Dawson asserts, "and far short of being able to build a genuine movement for democracy and justice." Other questions: Is black politics today less effective or ineffective. Or, should there be a different measure of effectiveness? It seems this new wave of awareness is battling against the tides of complacency and inactivity. While there is a loud noise of complaint rising from the community, the black community must become more actively aware.

In some, President Obama's 2008 election win produced the false expectation of an overwhelmingly positive impact on race relations. The election of the first African-American president did birth a new hope into the community, especially the children. However, according to Dawson, with the election came a false sense of security in the two party system. In 2009 and 2010 "African-Americans began to get much more discouraged...[upon] realizing President Obama's hands were ties" in many ways.

When asked about the possible racial implications of having who was a "viable" black presidential candidate in Herman Cain, Dawson clearly expressed the increased comfort of white Americans in their thinking. Those previously labeled as racist or at minimal racially biased, who happen to support Herman Cain use the fact of their support to "prove" race is not an issue. However, Dawson says, "[There is] a coarsening of racial rhetoric...People are much more empowered to say things which were [previously] out of bound." "Herman Cain has filled a gap on the socially conservative right that no one has been able to keep a grip on," Dawson continues to discuss the view of Herman Cain within the republican party, "He's there, he's black, we'll make use of it." Strategically, the expectation was that Herman Cain would rise as far as he had. Sexual harassment accusations aside, Cain's race was an issue. Some viewed the Republican Party as choosing the lesser of what they view as two evils. They either have a black democrat as president or support a black conservative republican. The racial tension in actuality cancels itself out. Herman Cain's race forced all parties and races to return their focus to the issue of economy, homeland security, and healthcare.

African-Americans must continue to push past the labels of "radicalism" and "militancy" and continue to demand justice and equality. Dawson says, "We [must] not let other people define us." The key to riding this racial wave is to remember that we are all Americans. We are all in the same economic boat. We are all facing unemployment, increased homelessness, and increased poverty levels. We all, regardless of the color of our skin, need to support our troops abroad who only care about the three colors that make up the American flag.

Racism is a fact. Brushed under the rug long enough, racial tension will seethe as an unattended infected wound. There is an economic and racial divide in America. At times, they are one in the same. Black politics has always been vocal and active not one of complacency or complaint. Dawson's book is a call to action. The truth hurt, but the truth heals.

Black Faces in White Places: 10 Game-Changing Strategies to Achieve Success and Find Greatness By Drs. Randal Pinkett and Jeffrey Robinson

In an earlier chapter, I stressed the importance of "excellence not excuses." Excellence is a game changer! When dealing with inequality connected to race, gender, disability, or sexuality, there is one sure way to overcome and overtake – EXCELLENCE! The book, Black Faces in White Places: 10 Game-Changing Strategies to Achieve Success and Find Greatness, by Drs. Randal Pinkett and Jeffrey Robinson are abundantly clear about how to change the game and position oneself for success. Politics and the black community can be considered frenemies. Both constantly at odds; yet, both need one another in order to implement desired change or prevent undesired change.

Defining Moments...Excellence...Education...Identity... Purpose...Community...The aforementioned themes are the foundation of the authors' game changing strategy. Initially, some readers may be concerned about the title, message, and intended audience. One may assume "angry" black men blaming "the man " or "the system" wrote the book. On the contrary, the book requires and equips one to look within. There is a common phrase, "Don't hate the player hate the game." Drs. Pinkett and Robinson encourage the reader to hate neither the player nor the game. Instead, learn one's own strengths and weaknesses as to become a stronger, strategic, player who understands the game at a high level.

The book makes it evident that making a choice is a necessity. One can sit on the sidelines and complain, play with an injured spirit, or get in the game with a strategy that will effectively change how one plays the game." Drs. Pinkett and Robinson give a remarkably concrete plan for strategically planning a life of success – better yet – greatness. In order to be an agent of change, one must first be an effective agent. The authors offer a plan for mind-set change and not shallow or superficial rhetoric.

As the title plainly states, there are 10 strategies. Most notable: Demonstrating Excellence, Thinking and Acting Intrapreneurially/Entrepreneurially, and Give back Generously. Of excellence, the authors "believe excellence is achieved when you bring empowering beliefs and old fashioned discipline to the intersection of your true passion and God-given gifts" (Pp.62-63). Of all the strategies in the book, excellence dominates. They challenge he reader to know and establish ones identity. Once done, excellence becomes the tool to facilitate perpetual success. The other nine strategies would fail if not executed with excellence of mind, body, and spirit.

This book, though addressed to the African-American population, is a powerful tool for all who face glass ceilings, career roadblocks, and political challenges. Advancement is connected to education and excellence. The book says little about the "plight of the black man/woman" except to identify the game, players, and the rules. It focuses on success rather than inequality and negative expectations.

If followed, the book equips the reader with many mental, spiritual, and social exercises educating the reader on how to push beyond acceptance, complacency, excuses, and mediocrity. Black Faces in White Places: 10 Game-Changing Strategies to Achieve Success and Find Greatness is a call to action – "DO BETTER and here is how."

9/11/01 A Long Road Toward Recovery

It is important to remember the victims, survivors, and families of September 11, 2001. We must never allow their voices fade - for they are the voices of freedom. They are the voices that remind us of the need to protect our freedoms. They are the voices who remind us to celebrate life every day because in a single moment living and life can change or disappear forever.

Here is the voice of Nicole B. Simpson, a 9/11 survivor and advocate:

> *"Facing death almost always forces an individual to assess what is really important in life. My story is no different. My name is Nicole B. Simpson and I am a World Trade Center survivor. My life was totally fulfilled and I was achieving the American dream on September 10, 2001. But the next day changed everything. I worked on the 73rd floor in Tower II although I felt the impact of Tower I being hit, I was not concerned until I looked out the window and saw burning paper similar to confetti at a NY Yankees Parade. I knew we had to get out of the building. Truthfully speaking, it was divine intervention that prompted me to move.*

> *I gathered my team and began to walk down the steps comforted by the continual announcement made through the public announcement system stating our tower was secure and we did not have to evacuate the building. When I arrived on the 44th floor, I stepped onto the elevator but felt the Lord telling me to stay where I was. I immediately got off the elevator and allowed the doors to close without me or my team.*

> *Approximately 30 seconds later, Tower II was hit and the elevators came crashing down causing fireball explosions to burn people standing along the elevator path. But the door that I was standing in front of did not open. Moments later I felt a release to move toward the stairs*

again to attempt evacuation. I ultimately left the building and that day changed the course of my life forever.

In the immediate aftermath, I was so grateful to be alive. I thought with my experience and expertise, I would be capable of rebounding in business. I didn't consider sleepless nights, physical pain, flashbacks and severe depression in the equation. Although I had accumulated savings, without a consistent income, my family endured serious financial hardship after one year. Physically, I began to deal with uneven breathing, lack of sleep and constant nightmares. I went to a counselor but I couldn't shake the feeling of guilt and anger. My life was fine-why me? I even thought about the fact that my family wouldn't suffer financially had I not survived.

I floundered in my field until I hit rock bottom in 2007 which was a year filled with disappointment and pain. Finally, I reached the point of no return. A decision had to be made. Was I going to allow September 11th 2001 to keep me in bondage or would I move forward? I made the decision that I would live. I would not allow 9/11 to defeat me and I would no longer participate in the category of the walking dead. I would no longer allow trauma and catastrophic events to steal my future because I was in the middle of America's worst terrorist attack.

My liberation didn't happen overnight. It began with a speech I gave titled Dare 2 Dream. While preparing the speech, I began to dream again. I decided to speak to people who suffered from catastrophic and traumatic events to encourage them to not allow their situations to define their future. In encouraging others, a spark was ignited in me. Today I still suffer from bouts of depression, anxiety and stress but I simply continue to dream new dreams.

Why am I sharing this with you? ...[As] a survivor, I have watched people dissect conspiracy theories, I have seen the media constantly rehash the day preventing individuals who were directly affected from healing. I have watched this national tragedy become more about politics and less about the people. But what was most distressing is that the survivors have been neglected and discarded.

For years, people who were in the buildings suffered in silence. Unfortunately, Pennsylvania was not exempt. People died on United Airlines Flight 93 yet where is the compassion for the families of the ones lost on that day? Significant emphasis has been placed on the families of the deceased and the first responders who risked their lives to save people like me. But does the fact that I did not lose my life justify that opportunity was stolen from me.

But hope has emerged. This year has brought about significant change. People are tired of war, they are hurting economically and they want to move forward. The capture of Osama Bin Ladin, the face of terrorism, added to the healing process for the country and the Zadroga Act signed into law provides opportunity for people to recover economically. So as we reflect on this last decade, I implore you to remember the survivors. To the residents of Pennsylvania and New Jersey, know that help is on the way!"

Listen attentively to Nicole's voice. As the country remembers that fateful day, listen to the silence – a space once filled with the voices of mothers, fathers, daughters, and sons.

Listen to the voices of the survivors, first responders, demolition and salvage teams, neighborhood families, and rebuilding teams who suffer from residual illnesses (mental and physical). Support the troops who immediately and continuously fight to ensure the United States will not have to listen to such silence (the piercing absence of mass voices) again! We as a nation stand with one voice saying "I AM MORE!"

Nicole B. Simpson, CFP represents the survivors. She spent almost three years talking to individuals directly impacted by the tragedy of 9/11/2001. In June, 2011, she released the survivor's story titled 9/11/01 A Long Road Toward Recovery. For further information on the life and ministry of Nicole, please contact Harvest Wealth Media Group at 732-377-2024 or email Nicole@nicolebsimpson.com

Not the Conclusion

M ost books include a chapter entitled "Conclusion," or the like. Every beginning has an ending. Books are no different. This book is no different. However, the conclusion is not in this book. This book is about my life. My complete story is not in this book. To add, the book cannot have a conclusion because my life has not concluded. I am still living. I am still surviving. Is that not what the book is about, surviving survival?

Post-Survival Affirmations

o *Saying "I AM MORE!" is saying:* I am no longer a product of my past; I am a facilitator of my future!

o *Saying "I AM MORE!" is saying:* I will not let the hurtful people from my past infect the people in my present that could effect and affect those in my future.

o *Saying "I AM MORE!" is saying:* It is my responsibility to use natural resources wisely, be a guiding light to those younger than I, contribute to the stability of my local economy, share stories of my achievements to encourage others, share stories of my failures to forewarn others, and express my love to those I love.

o *Saying "I AM MORE!" is saying:* I declare my independence TODAY! I am no longer dependent on those who abuse me to uplift me. I am not longer dependent on the drugs that are destroying me to strengthen me. I am no longer dependent on hatred and envy to motivate me. I declare independence from all forms of negativity. I WILL STAND STRONG AND FREE!

o *Saying "I AM MORE!" is saying:* I will only surrender to God and to the greatness He infused in me. I will not bow to complacency. I will not bow to lack. I will not bow to those who tell me that I am less than. I will not bow to addiction. I will not bow to sickness. I will not bow to corrupt education. I will stand before them declaring, "I AM MORE!"

o *Saying "I AM MORE!" is saying:* Just because you try to trip me does not mean you will make me fall. I have balance. I walk with each step planned and planted firmly.

o *Saying "I AM MORE!" is saying:* I walk with insight and foresight, refusing to be delayed by dwelling in hindsight.

Insight helps me to move forward. Foresight helps me to step over. Hindsight, in a glance, reminds me of lessons I learned. I have vision. I have a vision. I am a vision.

o *Saying "I AM MORE!" is saying:* I will dream. I will know when it is time to awaken from the dream. I will actively make the dream a reality. I will use my reality to invest in the dreams of another.

o *Saying "I AM MORE!" is saying:* I will not be held up or held back

o *Saying "I AM MORE!" is saying:* I will no longer simply pride myself in my ability to get a job, but in my ability to keep one.

o *Saying "I AM MORE!" is saying:* I will educate myself in how to educate others

o *Saying "I AM MORE!" is saying:* I will base my decisions, not on another's judgment of me, but, on my assessment of me and my future

o *Saying "I AM MORE!" is saying:* If you feel as though your past is forever before you (in front of you, blocking you) – you are facing the wrong way – TURN AROUND and face your future, not your past.

o *Saying "I AM MORE!" is saying:* I lift my eyes to the hills – the place of my help, grace, and sufficiency

o *Saying "I AM MORE!" is saying:* Tormentors can only be tormentors when I allow those people, thoughts, memories, and images to torment me.

o *Saying "I AM MORE!" is saying:* I am who I am, not who I was, and I am in constant preparation for who I was predestined to become

o *Saying "I AM MORE!" is saying:* I will not settle! Nor, will I be the one someone else settles for.

o *Saying "I AM MORE!" is saying:* I am a gifted gift that was given to this world so I can give

- *Saying "I AM MORE!" is saying:* I strive for excellence and trust God for perfection. I do not have to stress myself trying to be perfect.
- *Saying "I AM MORE!" is saying:* I will expand my mind & heart so God can expand my territory
- *Saying "I AM MORE!" is saying:* I will treat my body with love and respect because within it exists excellence, greatness, faithfulness, integrity, wisdom
- : *Saying "I AM MORE!" is saying:* Despite the loss of lives, we will not lose hope. Despite the destruction of our tangible memories, we will not surrender our future. Despite the great tragedy, we will resurrect a nation stronger, greater, and more prosperous than before.
- *Saying "I AM MORE!" is saying:* We are all brothers and sisters regardless of race, color, culture, or nationality. I AM MORE is a collective. It is not just "I" the individual. It is "I" the community – "I" the nation – "I" the world.
- *Saying "I AM MORE!" is saying:* I will not allow an economic recession to cause a mental depression
- *Saying "I AM MORE!" is saying:* I will dream. I will know when it is time to awaken from the dream. I will actively make the dream a reality. I will use my reality to invest in the dreams of another.
- *Saying "I AM MORE!" is saying:* You will respect me because I am respectable. I take responsibility for my role in the level of respect others have for me.
- *Saying "I AM MORE!" is saying:* Greatness is my birthright.
- *Saying "I AM MORE!" is saying:* It is in my emptiness and moments of brokenness that I have the greatest opportunity to become more. I will not waste those moments by expecting less (failure).

o *Saying "I AM MORE!" is saying:* Faith is the substance of things hoped for and the evidence of things not seen (Hebrews 11:1) I AM MORE whether you can see it or not – have faith. He (God) is more, so I am more.
o *Saying "I AM MORE!" is saying:* I am more than the sum of my bank accounts. Even if my accounts are in the negative, I will live in the positive.
o *Saying "I AM MORE!" is saying:* Who you thought you knew is not who I am. And, if you wait too long, the person you see will be gone. I AM MORE!
o *Saying "I AM MORE!" is saying:* I will not allow you to break me. I am stronger than you will ever know. I just might be stronger than I know.
o *Saying "I AM MORE!" is saying:* I will not allow you to dismiss me as a statistic.
o *Saying "I AM MORE!" is saying:* I will not be oppressed by your success.
o *Saying "I AM MORE!" is saying:* You cannot limit my "MORE"
o *Saying "I AM MORE!" is saying:* I will not apologize for telling you that you cannot go with me into my future.
o *Saying "I AM MORE!" is saying:* Of course, I am over-qualified. I have to be.
o *Saying "I AM MORE!" is saying:* It is my responsibility to be an asset to my community – an element of growth, not a hindrance.
o *Saying "I AM MORE!" is saying:* I do not need to put down another (person, area, race, sexuality, etc) to have pride in myself.
o *Saying "I AM MORE!" is saying:* My destiny is an extension of my predestination. I was created with a purpose. I will live up to and live out my purpose.

o *Saying "I AM MORE!" is saying:* I realize l am a part of a global community. Knowing that, I will make a positive contribution to society.

o *Saying "I AM MORE!" is saying:* I will give my children the love they need and the love they want, so they do not seek love from negative sources.

o *Saying "I AM MORE!" is saying:* it is okay to hurt, but it is not okay to be hindered by my pain. I will deal with and work through my pain so I can arrive at a place of healing.

o *Saying "I AM MORE!" is saying:* I will make my decisions based on evidence and fact not just emotion.

o *Saying "I AM MORE!" is saying:* My address does not define me. I am who I am not where I live.

o *Saying "I AM MORE!" is saying:* (To a significant other or family member) I see the 'more' in you and I want to help you nurture it.

o *Saying "I AM MORE!" is saying:* I will voluntarily submit to authority while not allowing myself to be oppressed by it.

o *Saying "I AM MORE!" is saying:* I will pay attention to my leader(s) so I can learn how to (or how not to) lead.

o *Saying "I AM MORE!" is saying:* it is time to control my impulses.

o *Saying "I AM MORE!" is saying:* I choose success.

o *Saying "I AM MORE!" is saying:* it is time to step out of my comfort zone allowing myself to mature and my territory to expand.

o *Saying "I AM MORE!" is saying:* I cannot do this alone. I need God, family, friends, and anyone who will be an active and effective source of power for me.

o *Saying "I AM MORE!" is saying:* My community needs me.

o *Saying "I AM MORE!" is saying:* I already survived, so I know I can live.
o *Saying "I AM MORE!" is saying:* I will speak about my accomplishments just as readily as I have spoken about pain and failures.
o *Saying "I AM MORE!" is saying:* While there are things I wish I had not said or did or allowed to happen, I will not dwell on what was done. Instead, I will focus on what I can do to turn them into foundations for my future.
o *Saying "I AM MORE!" is saying:* I will not allow my child(ren) to inherit my bitterness.
o *Saying "I AM MORE!" is saying:* My work product is an extension of me. I will produce and deliver excellence.
o *Saying "I AM MORE!" is saying:* No one can steal my joy or my smile or my pride.
o *Saying "I AM MORE!" is saying:* As the best, I am worthy of the best.
o *Saying "I AM MORE!" is saying:* I will take an active role in the strengthening of my marriage/relationship.
o *Saying "I AM MORE!" is saying:* Depression was a pitstop, not a destination. I'm going to keep it moving!
o *Saying "I AM MORE!" is saying:* I will not let you come between me and my child(ren).
o *Saying "I AM MORE!" is saying:* I do not have it all figured out...but for now that is ok.
o *Saying "I AM MORE!" is saying:* I am a friend of God
o *Saying "I AM MORE!" is saying:* I love me enough to let you see who I am.
o *Saying "I AM MORE!" is saying:* No one can steal my joy or my smile or my pride.
o *Saying "I AM MORE!" is saying:* As the best, I am worthy of the best.

○ *Saying "I AM MORE!" is saying:* I do not have to do things for the sole purpose of getting attention.
○ *Saying "I AM MORE!" is saying:* I love, appreciate, and respect myself. This qualifies me to love, appreciate, and respect others.
○ *Saying "I AM MORE!" is saying:* I can choose to start "new" life at any moment. I do not have to wait until the New Year's, a birthday, the start of the school year, or any other calendar defined day to turn my life in a more positive direction.
○ *Saying "I AM MORE!" is saying:* I refuse to remain addicted (actively abusing my body through drugs, alcohol, sex, overeating, work overload, too much television, etc).
○ *Saying "I AM MORE!" is saying:* I AM MORE! And, no one can tell me anything different!
○ *Saying "I AM MORE!" is saying:* I will introduce people to where I am going before explaining where I came from.
○ *Saying "I AM MORE!" is saying:* I will vote in local, school board, and primary elections to bring active change, improvement, or continued growth to my community.
○ *Saying "I AM MORE!" is saying:* Even if I only have one pair of pants, I will be clean, pressed, and confident. I will wear those pants every day with gratitude. It is not about people knowing what I do not have, it is about them see what I do with what I do have.
○ *Saying "I AM MORE!" is saying:* This is the day! Tomorrow will be the day, too! I will ask for help if necessary. I will do what it takes to make today a solid foundation for tomorrow.
○ *Saying "I AM MORE!" is saying:* I will be a leader who will not let my past effect the future of those I lead. I will lead them into their future, proud that I will one day be part of the great past that lead to a greater future.

o *Saying "I AM MORE!" is saying:* I know just enough to know I need to know more. I will not become complacent with my level of knowledge or education. The more I know I know, the more I want to know. The more I want to know, the more I will learn.

o *Saying "I AM MORE!" is saying:* There are times when I need to motivate myself. I can look to others for inspiration, but it is up me to move toward action and to act.

o *Saying "I AM MORE!" is saying:* I AM happy! I am willing to be happy!

o *Saying "I AM MORE!" is saying:* Is what this appears to be, actually what it is? Is this as serious as I am making it out to be?

o *Saying "I AM MORE!" is saying:* I love me. I appreciate me. I accept me. I do not worship me. My worship is reserved for God.

o *Saying "I AM MORE!" is saying:* Today I will laugh. Despite what I am going through – I will laugh. I will not laugh at the expense of another, but I will laugh in such a way as to be contagious.

o *Saying "I AM MORE!" is saying:* I will not quit. I will not settle. I will not stop.

o *Saying "I AM MORE!" is saying:* I use life's difficulties and obstacles as reasons to succeed rather than excuses to justify failure.

o *Saying "I AM MORE!" is saying:* I will make it. Whether I run, sprint, jog, walk, limp, hop, crawl, slide, or roll, I WILL MAKE IT. I AM MORE! This will not beat me.

o *Saying "I AM MORE!" is saying:* Your discomfort when your around me will not affect my comfort with who I am.

o *Saying "I AM MORE!" is saying:* I do not mind you being around because soon you will see the success you said I never would become.

o *Saying "I AM MORE!" is saying:* I am talented. I am resourceful. I am intelligent. I am a source of strength. I am a unique creation of God. I am living in excellence. I am wise. I am funny. I am comfortable with who I am. I am at peace with my past.

o *Saying "I AM MORE!" is saying:* I will accept my responsibility to make a positive contribution to my community. My community needs me in order for the community as a whole to say "I AM MORE!" in unison. Simply restating the problems are no longer enough for me. I will invest time, money, energy, expertise, and/or wisdom in to my community.

o *Saying "I AM MORE!" is saying:* I will tell myself the truth about me. I refuse to live in denial. I can only be 'more' if I acknowledge the truth about where and who I am now.

o *Saying "I AM MORE!" is saying:* I may be sad, disappointed, or upset, but these feelings are only temporary. I can and will overcome even my own emotions.

o *Saying "I AM MORE!" is saying:* I AM MORE because I was created as such. The more I am – the more I will become. I will not accept the lie: "you are nothing." I was created out of nothing. I was not created as "nothing".

o *Saying "I AM MORE!" is saying:* I will embrace change if it means progress. I will create change if it means success.

o *Saying "I AM MORE!" is saying:* I can help you with your problem without making it my problem. I am here to assist, not to absorb.

o *Saying "I AM MORE!" is saying:* I will no longer be my own stumbling block. I will get over myself. I will step up and keep on stepping.

o *Saying "I AM MORE!" is saying:* There are no shortcuts to greatness. Greatness is who I am (my character, my attitude, my spirituality, etc) not what I am (my profession, my grades, my financial status, etc.).

o **Saying "I AM MORE!" is saying:** (As a business owner) I will focus on providing a quality service or a product. I will treat my clients/customers with respect and not as if I am doing them a favor. The want/need my product or service, and I want/need their patronage.

o **Saying "I AM MORE!" is saying:** When everything around me seems dark, I will consider it my chance to truly shine.

o **Saying "I AM MORE!" is saying:** I will not discount my worth.

o **Saying "I AM MORE!" is saying:** I have been through so much that I have to see how this all plays out. My life is like a movie, and I will not leave until the Creator says: "THE END". Until that time, I will play my role with excellence and integrity.

o **Saying "I AM MORE!" is saying:** Faith is all I have. So, I'm glad faith is all I need.

o **Saying "I AM MORE!" is saying:** I am too proud to ask for help, so I will request assistance.

o **Saying "I AM MORE!" is saying:** I am addicted. I am recovering. I am free. In each phase, I AM MORE!

o **Saying "I AM MORE!" is saying:** I know I can do anything. The only thing I cannot do is give up.

o **Saying "I AM MORE!" is saying:** I am no longer afraid of my own greatness. I am comfortable with my future successes. I can do this.

o **Saying "I AM MORE!" is saying:** I am working too hard to stay afloat; I might as well use the same energy to swim to shore.

o **Saying "I AM MORE!" is saying:** I will dream. I will know when it is time to awaken from the dream. I will actively make the dream a reality. I will use my reality to invest in the dreams of another.

o *Saying "I AM MORE!" is saying:* I will not settle! Nor, will I be the one someone else settles for.

o *Saying "I AM MORE!" is saying:* It is in my emptiness and moments of brokenness that I have the greatest opportunity to become more. I will not waste those moments by expecting less (failure).

o *Saying "I AM MORE!" is saying:* It is my responsibility to be an asset to my community – an element of growth, not a hindrance.

o *Saying "I AM MORE!" is saying:* My boss may be responsible for my promotion, but I am responsible for my advancement. They can decide not to promote me, but I can still work toward my own advancement. Advancement is transferrable to another job or career.

o *Saying "I AM MORE!" is saying:* I understand I will not know how much 'more' I am until I take the time to assess myself. I need to pause when it comes to bringing out the best in others so I can concentrate on presenting to the world the greatness in me.

o *Saying "I AM MORE!" is saying:* I will celebrate the accomplishments of others as if it were my own. I will not minimize the achievement of friends, family, or co-workers because I have not YET achieved what I desire for myself.

o *Saying "I AM MORE!" is saying:* No one can read my mind. So, I take full responsibility for relaying my feelings to those whom I feel need to know and understand them.

o *Saying "I AM MORE!" is saying:* I know just enough to know I need to know more. I will not become complacent with my level of knowledge or education. The more I know, the more I want to know. The more I want to know, the more I will learn.

o *Saying "I AM MORE!" is saying:* I will not spend my time analyzing why people wronged me. I will not sit and reflect on loose ends. I realize the answers may never come or may reveal themselves with time. I will instead live. I will experience more love, more happiness, and more memories.

o *Saying "I AM MORE!" is saying:* I am a child, but I AM MORE! I am more than just your responsibility, I am your investment. I am more than just your offspring; I am the board off which the future will spring. I am not your sequel, I am my own beginning.

o *Saying "I AM MORE!" is saying:* When I look in the mirror I see more than I saw yesterday. I am glad to know it is not as much as I will see tomorrow. In being more, I know that I will be more.

o *Saying "I AM MORE!" is saying:* I will not be consumed by my own appetite. I can and will only take on healthy portions of food, sex, work, adventure, or anything else for which I crave. I know a healthy appetite is a key ingredient for a healthy lifestyle.

o *Saying "I AM MORE!" is saying:* I will be true to myself and real with others. I will not hide my true identity under a Wonder Woman, Iron Man, or Superman suit. I am not invincible, and I will not allow myself to get hurt because I am trying to prove that I am so.

o *Saying "I AM MORE!" is saying:* I can and will keep my word. I recognize that if I tell someone I will do something and do not, I lied. I want others to see me as a person of integrity, strong values, and ethics. What I say has an impact on the lives of others. Not doing what I said I would do has an impact on how others see me.

o *Saying "I AM MORE!" is saying:* I love me. I respect me. I admire me. I am proud of me. I am filled with greatness. I am blessed to be me.

o *Saying "I AM MORE!" is saying:* I will not allow the negative expectations of others to impact my expectations of myself.

o *Saying "I AM MORE!" is saying:* You cannot stop me. You may delay me, but you cannot stop me. I will utilize my options and take detours around you. You think you are a road block, but you are only a speed bump.

o *Saying "I AM MORE!" is saying:* I will set myself apart as a leader. I will follow other leaders, not other followers.

o *Saying "I AM MORE!" is saying:* I will not measure my success by the success of others. Nor will I measure my future success by my past successes. I will measure each success on its own merit and according to its own time.

o *Saying "I AM MORE!" is saying:* I will stop making haphazard decisions. I will take time to strategize. I refuse to live through more situations that are undesirable simply because I did not have a plan.

o *Saying "I AM MORE!" is saying:* "All I do is win, win, win," - even when I lose. When I lose I will recognize I won strength, knowledge, understanding, and experience. Next time I face that same opponent, I will know what to expect and how to respond. I will look at myself always as victorious.

o *Saying "I AM MORE!" is saying:* I will peacefully live in peace. I will not start a war in my home as a way to solicit peace. The first mouth I can successfully shut is my own.

o *Saying "I AM MORE!" is saying:* I will keep my hands to myself. I will not reach out in anger to any man, woman, child, or animal. I will not harm myself. I will learn to verbalize (or write) my frustrations and anger. I AM MORE than the violence I feel.

- *Saying "I AM MORE!" is saying:* I understand the responsibility attached to my words. I will use my word to build rather than destroy. I will speak love rather than hate. I will nurture rather than torment. My words are tentacles which reach further than my arms could ever.
- *Saying "I AM MORE!" is saying:* I will enjoy life! In other words, I will usher 'in joy' to my life. I will not allow my hindsight nor my current place in life to suck the joy out of my life. I acknowledge joy is found in my heart and is timeless while happiness is in my mind and limited by time and circumstance.
- *Saying "I AM MORE!" is saying:* I will not let my actions contradict my words. I am who I say I am. I do what I say I do. I live how I say I live.
- *Saying "I AM MORE!" is saying:* I see the strengths in my faults more than the faults in my strengths.
- *Saying "I AM MORE!" is saying:* I survived so I can live.
- *Saying "I AM MORE!" is saying:* I am worth it! I am worth the love it takes to love me. I am worth the salary it takes to compensate me. I am worth the hope it takes to have faith in me. I am worth the strength it takes to protect me. I am worth the hug it takes to embrace me. I am worth the words it takes to correct me. I am worth the time it takes to be with me. I AM WORTH IT!
- *Saying "I AM MORE!" is saying:* I will not settle! Nor, will I be the one someone else settles for.
- *Saying "I AM MORE!" is saying:* I am more than the sum of my bank accounts. Even if my accounts are in the negative, I will live in the positive.
- *Saying "I AM MORE!" is saying:* I will use my power for good. I have the power to make this a good day. I have the

power to end an argument. I have the power to stay or leave. I have the power to laugh or cry. I have the power to speak live or death. It is in my power to change or remain stagnant.

o **Saying "I AM MORE!" is saying:** I will not walk down the middle of life's road fearing a step to either side will cause me to loss family or friends. Doing so puts me in danger of losing the essence of who I am. I will formulate, commit to, and stand on my own beliefs.

o **Saying "I AM MORE!" is saying:** I will dream. I will know when it is time to awaken from the dream. I will actively make the dream a reality. I will use my reality to invest in the dreams of another.

o **Saying "I AM MORE!" is saying:** I have been through so much that I have to see how this all plays out. My life is like a movie, and I will not leave until the Creator says: "THE END". Until that time, I will play my role with excellence and integrity.

o **Saying "I AM MORE!" is saying:** I declare freedom! I declare today I will not be a slave to depression, loneliness, anger, hatred, stress, lack, or any negativity. I declare my freedom from accepting oppression as part of my life. I am hereby free from addiction, pain, hurt, and degradation. My freedom starts first in my mind! Today I am free!

o **Saying "I AM MORE!" is saying:** I am strong. I have the strength in reserve for times like this. I'm going to blow a hole in this mountain I am facing and walk straight through it. I am strong enough to move on.

o *Saying "I AM MORE!" is saying: I am EXTRA-ordinary. This means I can perform extraordinary feats with ordinary resources. My mind has the ability to think up extraordinary ways to accomplish extraordinary successes. My faith, even through my weakest moments, is extraordinary. My extraordinary strength and faith combine with my extraordinary abilities and talents to make extraordinary strides in greatness.*

o *Saying "I AM MORE!" is saying:* I am a limited resource with unlimited possibilities. Like any precious (and priceless) resource, I must be used wisely. I will be wise in how I allow others to use me as a resource. I will not allow others to "use me up" and attempt to limit my possibilities while increasing theirs.

o *Saying "I AM MORE!" is saying:* I am a key part of every one of my relationships. It is up to me to take responsibility for the positive growth in the relationship. It is up to me to stop taking the negativity from previous relationships and reinvesting them in current relationships. It is up to me to do everything I can, including knowing when enough is enough, and it is time to move on.

o *Saying "I AM MORE!" is saying:* I have a voice. I will be heard. My actions are part of my voice. I will use my voice to promote myself rather than to cause my own defeat.

o *Saying "I AM MORE!" is saying:* This is a new day. Today is my day one. While I may have to live out the consequences and responsibilities of my past, today I will do so with a new mindset. Today is the beginning of a new strength.

o *Saying "I AM MORE!" is saying:* I will take full responsibility for my actions. I will recognize, acknowledge, and hold myself accountable for the consequences of my actions. No one else is responsible for what I do, say, or set in motion but me.

o *Saying "I AM MORE!" is saying:* There are things which happened to me and things that happened because of me. There are things that were done to me and things I did. I recognize and own up to my responsibility for my current station in life. I will not longer blame others for my failures knowing if I succeeded I would not have credited them for those successes.

- o *Saying "I AM MORE!" is saying:* I will eliminate descriptions such as hopeless, useless, and nothing from my assessment of my life and myself. I AM MORE! I will remove doubt, fear, and anger from my emotional cache. I AM MORE. I will stand in hope, faith, love, freedom, strength, power, loyalty, and victory because "I AM MORE!"
- o *Saying "I AM MORE!" is saying:* Silence is golden, but peace is platinum. I know the difference between silence and peace.
- o *Saying "I AM MORE!" is saying:* Being pleased with who I am makes it easier for others to please me. I will be more available for pleasure and more willing to smile.
- o *Saying "I AM MORE!" is saying:* I will not be imprisoned by my own successes. I will not allow today's success to limit me from future successes. I will continue to strive for higher levels of greatness.
- o *Saying "I AM MORE!" is saying:* Me being single may not be because I was not "the one". It
- o *Saying "I AM MORE!" is saying:* I AM MORE! That is it...I AM MORE! Whatever you think of me...I AM MORE! Whatever you see...I AM MORE! Whatever I have done...I AM MORE! I AM MORE! I AM MORE! I AM MORE!
- o *Saying "I AM MORE!" is saying:* Pressure can break me or it can turn me into a diamond. I know I am diamond material so I will NOT break.
- o *Saying "I AM MORE!" is saying:* I will not covet my neighbor's anything. What is for them is for them. What is for me, is for me. I will have what is intended for me in

time. Coveting what someone else has only wastes time that can be spent pursuing my own.

o   *Saying "I AM MORE!" is saying:* I am more than my criminal record. My criminal history is just that – history! It is a record of my past mistakes. It says NOTHING about my future

o   *Saying "I AM MORE!" is saying:* I will stop giving away pieces of me so I can retain peace in me.

o   *Saying "I AM MORE!" is saying:* "I am no longer a product of my past; I am a facilitator of my future." I am not a finished product. I am ever growing and evolving. My future is a product of me; I am not simply a product of my past.

o   *Saying "I AM MORE!" is saying:* My faith is my vaccination against fear. I will have faith in God. I will have faith in my future. I will have faith in the next steps I will take. I will have faith in me. I will not fear.

o   *Saying "I AM MORE!" is saying:* "Faith is the substance of things hoped for and the evidence of things not seen" (Hebrews 11:1) – I know that if I have less faith, I have less hope. Since there is no hopeless situation to God, I will be faith-full, knowing I will make it through this.

o   *Saying "I AM MORE!" is saying:* Dear Self, – You are imperfect. You make mistakes from time to time (some are quite humorous). You seem to find new ways to get into troublesome situations. Yet, I find you the strongest, most fascinating person I know. I see you as simply amazing. I am blessed to know you. In fact, I want you to know – I love you! Signed, Me

o   *Saying "I AM MORE!" is saying:* The greatest thing I can do today is be great today.

o   *Saying "I AM MORE!" is saying:* I stand strong as a father. I recognize and accept my importance in my children's lives. I am blessed that my role comes without an expiration date. I am proud to be a 'daddy'.

o *Saying "I AM MORE!" is saying:* I will not allow society to define me in the eyes of my children. They will know me for who I am and not by what the media reports. I will be a role model and not a validation to the negative statistics and stereo-types. I am an extremely valuable part of their foundation. I will re-enforce their greatness.

o *Saying "I AM MORE!" is saying:* I am great with my greatness. I will be true to myself and my beliefs.

o *Saying "I AM MORE!" is saying:* I will not force the people in my present to be condemned for the wrongdoings of those in my past. I will learn to trust.

o *Saying "I AM MORE!" is saying:* I am empowered by God. I am a source of power which points to the Power Source that is God. As long as I am plugged in to God, I will have the power and strength I need.

o *Saying "I AM MORE!" is saying:* I will not blame God when I make a mistake and He does not get me out of it.

o *Saying "I AM MORE!" is saying:* It is my responsibility to contribute positively to my local and global community. I am not just existing, I am coexisting. I will not walk around as if I am the ruler of my own world. I will recognize the needs of the community and do SOMETHING to bring attention to and/or fulfill those needs. It is my responsibility to understand that it is not all about me.

o *Saying "I AM MORE!" is saying:* I will not continue to hide my greatness behind laziness, irresponsibility, addiction, lack of education, or disrespect. I will allow my greatness to shine rather than be overshadowed. I have no control over what people see, but full control over what I show them.

- o *Saying "I AM MORE!" is saying:* There is only one way to live and that is to live. I will take responsibility for my living. God is responsible for my life. It is my responsibility to live my life. I will not delegate that responsibility to my parents, my spouse, my employer, my teacher, the banks, or anyone else. I control how I live.
- o *Saying "I AM MORE!" is saying:* I will not continue to hide my greatness behind laziness, irresponsibility, addiction, lack of education, or disrespect. I will allow my greatness to shine rather than be overshadowed. I have no control over what people see, but full control over what I show them.
- o *Saying "I AM MORE!" is saying:* You will not get me down today. I am here for you, to support you, even to pray for you. But, I will not let your life stress to stress my life. I turn down your invitation to the pity party you planned. I am not available for man/woman bashing. I will only speak of problems if we are also planning solutions. I will enjoy my day.

References

Dawson, M. C. (2011). *Not in Our Lifetimes: The Future of Black Politics.* Chicago: University of Chicago Press.

Pinckney, T. M. (2009). *I Am More - the Journey.* Tulsa, OK: Total Publishing and Media.

Pinckney, T. M. (2011, August 27). 9/11: 10 Years Later, A Survivor Speaks. Retrieved from http://www.examiner.com/article/9-11-10-years-later-a-survivor-speaks

Pinkett, R., & Robinson, J. (2011). *Black Faces in White Places: 10 Game-Changing strategies to Achieve Success and Find Greatness.* New York: American Management Association.

Simpson, N. B. (2001). *9/11/01 A Long Road Toward Recovery.* New Jersey: Harvest Wealth Media Group.

Trulson, C. R. (2005). Victims' Rights and Services: Eligibility, Exclusion, and Victim Worth. *Criminology & Public Policy, 4*(2), 399-414.

Weitzman, S. (2000). *Not to People Like Us: Hidden Abuse in Upscale Marriages.* New York: Basic Books.

Weizman, S., Rankin, D., Martin, B., Dawson, M., Simpson, N., & Langbein, J. (September 2011-January 2012). Various Interviews to Obtain Information for Articles on Domestic Violence, African-American Politics and Entrepreneurs, and September 11, 2001. (T. M. Pinckney, Interviewer) Retrieved from http://www.tonishapinckney.com/Awareness.html

About the Author

S aying "I AM MORE!" is the gateway to living your best life! Tonisha "Ms. Toni" Pinckney took these three simple words and embarked on a life transforming journey. It is her life purpose to remind people "you are no longer a product of your past; you are a facilitator of your future!" Ms. Toni teaches, it is the realization that you are more, you are capable of more, and you are worthy of more that will launch you into a powerfully productive future. It is excellence not excuses that equips people to live their best life. Through seminars, lectures, community events, personal partnering, writing, and various other methods of communication, Ms. Toni empowers and transforms lives, communities, and organizations. She transforms lives into legacies!

Professionally, Ms. Toni is a certified fraud examiner and certified forensic financial analyst with a specialty in forensic accounting and investigative methodologies. The certifications support her formal education: B.S. in Accounting (Kean University), M.S. in Criminal Justice (University of Cincinnati), Certificate in Forensic Criminology (University of Massachusetts), and a Certificate in Security Studies (University of Massachusetts). She also took Executive Leadership courses (Strategic Thinking and Executive Decision Making) via Cornell University. Currently, Ms. Toni is a Doctoral Teaching Fellow at the University of Massachusetts Lowell where she is completing her Ph.D. in Criminal Justice and Criminology. At UMASS Lowell, she is teaching Intimate Partner Violence and developing other courses.

Her experience and expertise allow her to participate in litigation and investigations connected to divorce proceedings, division of property issues, estate matters, fraud deterrence and detection issues and all other matters that require investigative accounting. She is a qualified trained expert witness. In recent years, Ms. Toni focused her abilities toward those in the sports and entertainment industries. Understanding the necessity of social responsibility and active awareness, Ms. Toni donates her time and expertise to advise victims, parents of children with challenges, those seeking to start a business in response to catastrophic life events, and churches or other non-profit organizations.

A single mother of two boys, Ms. Toni is the founding CEO of I AM MORE, LLC and Revelatus Specialized Accounting & Consulting (RSA Consulting), and the Visionary and Founder of I AM MORE Institute for Excellence & Social Responsibility, Inc (I AM MORE Institute). It was her personal experience that led Ms. Toni on a quest to become familiar with the complexities of criminology and victimology. A survivor of sexual assault, domestic violence, and emotional abuse, her story is one of "empowerment beyond victimization!" She lives the struggles of being a single mother, understands the emotional stress of living with a mentally ill family member, and sees the toll crime and economic lack has on the inner-city community. She uses that strength to help others spiritually, emotionally, and economically empower themselves. Her story covers almost the full span of human emotions and inspires others to live a life of "excellence not excuses" while "surviving survival."

Ms. Toni is a well-respected and sought after speaker, mentor, and transformation partner. Whether through one of her ventures, as a member of the Speakers' Bureau of RAINN (Rape, Abuse, Incest, National Network), or through her home church, Ms. Toni is requested to speak for schools (grades 3-12), universities, churches, organizations, radio and television programs, and various events. Understanding the power of testimony, Ms. Toni shares with all despite one's age, socio-economic standing, race, color, religion, sexuality, gender, education level, disability, victimizations, or offenses. The moment she said, "I AM MORE!" her life was forever transformed. It is through that transformation that she is empowered to help others transform their lives with the same three words. Tonisha "Ms. Toni" Pinckney is the author of *I AM MORE – the Journey,* and *I AM MORE – Surviving Survival.*

Contact Info: info@iammoreonline.com
Facebook: www.facebook.com/IAMMORE
Twitter: @IAMMORE (www.twitter.com/IAMMORE)
Website www.tonishapinckney.com/www.iammoreonline.com

CPSIA information can be obtained at www.ICGtesting.com
Printed in the USA
BVOW021654050313

314613BV00006B/13/P